TOWARD A MORE PERFECT UNION:
Basic Skills, Poor Families, and Our Economic Future

By Gordon Berlin and Andrew Sum

Occasional Paper Number Three
Ford Foundation Project on
Social Welfare and the American Future

Ford Foundation
New York, N.Y.

One of a series of reports on activities by the Ford
Foundation. A complete list of publications may be
obtained from the Ford Foundation, Office of Reports,
320 East 43 Street, New York, New York 10017.

Library of Congress Cataloging-in-Publication Data
Berlin, Gordon.
   Toward a more perfect union: basic skills, poor fam-
ilies, and our economic future/by Gordon Berlin and
Andrew Sum.
      p.   cm.—(Occasional paper/Ford Foundation,
Project on Social Welfare and the American Future; no. 3)
   Includes bibliographical references.
   ISBN 0-916584-32-1
   1. Basic education—Government policy—United
States.   2. Vocational education—Government policy—
United States.   3. Socially handicapped—Education—
United States.   4. United States—Social policy—1980–
5. United States—Economic policy—1981–   I. Sum,
Andrew. II. Title. III. Series: Occasional paper (Ford
Foundation. Project on Social Welfare and the American
Future); no. 3.
LC1035.6.B47 1988
371.96′7—dc19   87-33197
                                          CIP

464   February 1988
© 1988 Ford Foundation

Cover Photograph: Joe Viesti

Contents

Foreword

The United States has a two-pronged system of social welfare—one designed for labor-force participants and the other for those who do not work. For workers, a combination of employee benefits and government social insurance programs provides protection against the risks of illness, disability, and unemployment and also sets aside funds for income maintenance and health coverage during the retirement years. Nonworkers, mainly children, the disabled, and the elderly, are sustained by a governmental safety-net program. Except for low-income single parents with young children, able-bodied, working-age adults are expected to work and thereby provide for their needs.

Does this social welfare system, designed in large part in the 1930s, provide sufficient protection for Americans as they are about to enter the twenty-first century? Have significant holes developed in the fabric of social protection, and, if so, is society willing to pay for mending them? Has the changing composition of the U.S. population, specifically the increase in the elderly and single-parent families, altered the premises on which the system was built? Why is there such a persistently high level of poverty, in good times and bad, and can anything be done to correct it? Can more be done to help the troubling number of American children who experience at least some poverty in their growing-up years?

These are some of the questions that the Ford Foundation set out to answer when in 1985 it launched a wide-ranging inquiry into alternative approaches to providing social insurance and welfare services, taking into account changes in the economy, in the family and work, and in the nation's age profile. Called the Project on Social Welfare and the American Future, the inquiry is led by a twelve-member executive panel of citizens representing the business, academic, civil rights, and labor communities.* Chairman of the panel is Irving S. Shapiro, until recently a member of the Foundation's Board of Trustees and a former chief executive officer of the du Pont Company.

In the course of its inquiry, the panel has commissioned a number of research reports and convened sessions of social policy experts to discuss approaches to such interrelated topics as health care, retirement and pension policy, poverty and welfare policy, and public and private social welfare programs. For one of the sessions, in September 1986, the panel invited leading scholars and practitioners in the field of poverty and welfare to discuss the policy implications of their work. They were asked to address three topics: the diverse and interrelated causes of poverty, the consequences of poverty for individuals and society as a whole, and whether the safety-net and training programs developed since the 1930s are appropriate for fighting poverty in the 1980s and beyond.

Together with several specially commissioned research reports, the papers offer an unusually comprehensive picture of why people are poor and what has been and might be done about it. For this reason, the Foundation has decided to publish them. The first two, issued in November 1987, were David T. Ellwood's review of our various income-maintenance programs and Judith M. Gueron's paper on how the welfare system might be reformed. Now Gordon Berlin and Andrew Sum analyze the links between inadequate basic skills and a variety of social problems, from dropping out of school to unemployment to welfare dependency. Other papers will follow. The views expressed in the papers are the authors' own and do not necessarily reflect those of members of the executive panel or of the staff and board of the Ford Foundation.

We are grateful to the authors for taking time out from their busy schedules to set down their thoughts on a complex range of issues. Together, they have made a useful contribution to the current debate over social welfare policy.

Franklin A. Thomas
President
Ford Foundation

---

* Members of the panel are listed on page iii.

Acknowledgments

The authors wish to express their thanks to Robert Taggart and Frank Levy for their encouragement, insights, and guidance; to Sar Levitan and Tammy Mitchell for their substantive suggestions and editorial contributions; to Harold Howe III, Raymond Reisler, Barbara Heyns, and Barbara Nelson for their critical comments and advice; to Neal Fogg and William Goedicke for their research assistance; and to the many people in the Ford Foundation and at the September conference who made this report possible.

Introduction

In the 1980s and 1990s important demographic, economic, and social changes will affect the nation's schools, families, and workplaces. In anticipation of these developments, there is renewed interest in formal educational attainment and basic academic skills. The National Commission on Excellence in Education titled its report on the need for educational reform *A Nation at Risk: The Imperative for Educational Reform.*[1] The Panel on Adolescent Pregnancy and Childbearing of the National Research Council warned that the nation and its children are "risking the future." Noting that "inadequate basic skills, poor employment prospects and the lack of successful role models . . . have stifled the motivation of many to . . . avoid pregnancy," the panel placed its highest priority on preventing adolescent parenting by enhancing young people's life options.[2] In *Strategy for U.S. Industrial Competitiveness,* the Committee for Economic Development argued that the quality of education, especially at the pre-college level, will determine the ability of the labor force to adapt to changes resulting from new productivity-enhancing technologies.[3]

Each of these reports focuses on a critical and seemingly distinct national problem—inadequate schools, teenage parenting, and economic competitiveness. Yet they contain a common theme—the importance of basic academic skills. In this paper, we argue that a concerted national effort to address the current crisis in basic skills would advance the nation's goals in several important ways.

Why are basic skills important? Because those with better basic skills—defined as the ability to read, write, communicate, and compute—do better in school, at work, and in other key areas of their lives. They are more likely to perform well in school, obtain a high school diploma, go on to and complete college, work more hours, earn higher wages, be more productive workers, and avoid bearing children

1

out of wedlock. Conversely, those who are deficient in basic skills are more likely to be school dropouts, teenage parents, jobless, welfare dependent, and involved in crime. Moreover, in an interdependent world economy, the skills of the nation's work force are becoming an increasingly important determinant of American industry's competitive position, workers' real wages, and our overall standard of living. In short, basic skills bear a distinct relation to the future well-being of workers, families, firms, and the country itself.

Fortunately, improving the basic academic skills of American youth is a problem we can do something about. But we must know where to begin. Thus far, we have but dimly understood the problem. We have decried the "rising tide of mediocrity" in our schools without understanding the sources or consequences of that mediocrity. We have wrongly attributed the cause of poor achievement to the lack of innate ability rather than lack of effort. We have called for voluntary tutors, as if the nation's literacy problem was predominantly one of people who cannot read at all, when it is rather a problem of low levels of functional literacy and critical reasoning. We have worried about our ability to compete ("Can America Compete?"), often looking to global rather than domestic causes.[4] In fact, hardly a day passes without some newspaper or magazine referring to the competitiveness issue or to the ineptitude of our schools or to the ineffectiveness of our training programs. But clichés and assertions will not lead to right action. The first step is to understand the problem in its full complexity and the complete range of its economic and social implications.

This paper attempts to show how inadequate basic academic skills are intertwined with problems of youth employment and with dropping out of school, out-of-wedlock parenting, welfare dependency, and the decline in work-force productivity growth. The first section examines relations among macroeconomic trends, individual earnings, family-formation patterns, and educational achievement. The second explores the basic-skills crisis, presenting evidence that inadequate skills are an underlying cause of poverty and economic dependency, and identifying the intergenerational causes and consequences of inadequate basic skills. The third part presents a conceptual framework for thinking about the problem, describes effective programs, outlines a system for improving the quality of current programs and the accountability of the institutions involved, and identifies weaknesses in the nation's current educational and training institutions and systems. The final section suggests an agenda for future action.

The Economic Environment

We begin with a brief overview of key developments in the U.S. national economy. It may seem shocking, but many economists have used the words "recession" and "depression" to describe key aspects of our economic performance throughout most of the last decade and more. Between 1973 and 1984 median real family income actually fell; that is, after adjustments for inflation, the typical American family had somewhat less purchasing power in 1984 than it had in 1973.[5]

This development stands in stark contrast to the economic experience of American families during the three decades after World War II. Between 1947 and 1973 the annual median real income of American families (in 1984 dollars) increased from $14,095 to $28,167, representing a doubling of their purchasing power.[6] Yet by 1984 the median real income of American families stood at only $26,433, a figure more than 6 percent below that of 1973. Jimmy Carter agonized over this "malaise" in the midst of plenty, and Ronald Reagan denied it. Yet it is central to explaining what has happened to families' well-being, why poverty has been increasing, why out-of-wedlock births are rising, and why many Americans have had a change of heart about funding social programs.[7]

Falling Productivity and Stagnant Wages

To help us understand where we have been and where we may be going, several economists recently divided the postwar economy into two periods: before and after 1973. The year 1973 was both our last very good year and the beginning of many bad years in aggregate economic performance. It marked the first major OPEC oil price increase, the initial peak of the baby-boom cohort's movement into the work force, and an acceleration of the inflation that began with the guns-and-butter policies of the Vietnam War. Together, these developments signaled the transition from twenty-six years of sustained real wage growth to fifteen years of wage stagnation.[8]

It is worth noting that the economists who talked about this stagnation measured good or bad times according to wages and annual earnings rather than unemployment. Although unemployment has symbolized hard times since the Great Depression of the 1930s, rising real wages are increasingly important in the long run, since they signal rising productivity and affluence and act as a cushion in difficult times. If real wages are low, the unemployment of the primary earner may mean sudden poverty, but if real wages are high, a family may have adequate savings to get along for a few months. Real wages also determine how much purchasing power the average family has and thus its standard of living—the type of house it can afford, the number and quality of cars, recreational opportunities, the type of college education the children will get, and so forth. And, of course, a rising standard of living is the ultimate goal of economic growth.

Yet if real wages are to rise, the productivity of workers must also grow. During the twenty-six-year period from 1947 to 1973 labor productivity in the private sector—the amount of output produced by each worker per hour—grew at an annual rate of 2.5 percent to 3.0 percent.[9] With each worker producing more, real wages grew at about 3 percent a year. After the confluence of unlucky events that occurred in 1973, productivity growth rates in the nonfarm business sector fell precipitously to less than 1 percent a year.[10] As a result, real wage growth stagnated in most cases, and for many workers real wages actually declined.[11]

As Frank Levy has shown, the best way to understand what these developments have meant for American workers is to track the median real earnings of a typical man as he aged from forty to fifty in three different ten-year time periods.[12] In the pre-1973 period, despite the fact that most of his major promotions were behind him, Levy's typical man would almost inexorably see his real earnings grow 25 to 30 percent every ten years. At that time, unemployment rates were relatively low, labor productivity was steadily rising, and real wages and earnings followed suit. Levy imagines his typical worker on an ''up-escalator.'' He was not necessarily doing any better than his neighbors, but he was always doing better personally. If he lost his job but eventually got another one, it would not be very long before he was back at his previous level on the escalator.

But what happened after 1973? If Levy's typical man had the misfortune of aging from forty to fifty in the ten-year period from 1973 to 1983, his circumstances were very different. Rather than seeing his real earnings increase by 30 percent or so in those ten years, he saw them decline by 14 percent (see Figure 1). By the end of the decade, he had 44 percent less real income than he would have expected to have in any other postwar decade.

This "bad times" view of the economy of the 1970s may seem somewhat contradictory. Even though real wages and earnings were declining and the growth of real Gross National Product (GNP) per hour of work was rising more slowly, real GNP—the total value of the final goods and services produced by the economy adjusted for inflation—actually grew at 3.0 percent during the 1970s, a rate that even exceeded that of the 1950s. This rate of growth was well in excess of that of the population (1.0 percent). As a result, real GNP per man, woman, and child (per capita) was also growing.

How can we explain the paradox of a growing overall economy in the face of declining real wages? Part of the answer lies in the ingenuity of the American people. They kept their standard of living up even while individual real wages were falling by doing the following four things: they postponed marriage, both spouses entered the labor market,

Figure 1 Average ten-year real income gains for men passing from age 40 to age 50, U.S., 1950–1983

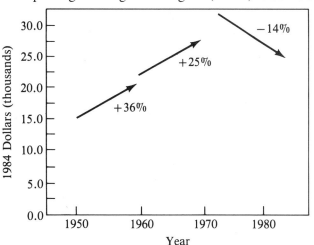

Source: Frank Levy, *Dollars and Dreams* (New York: Basic Books, 1987).

they had fewer children, and they went into debt.[13] With two or more people working per family and fewer children, families could maintain a high standard of living, even though the real earnings of their primary wage earner were declining. Thus, during the 1970s real GNP per worker basically remained unchanged, even though real GNP per person was growing. Taking into account lost leisure time, home output, and increased debt, these families were not living as well as their parents who had more children and frequently only one adult family member working. But the strategies of the 1970s and early 1980s had two important limitations: only two-parent families could take advantage of them, and they could use them only once. If all available earners are working and if a family already has fewer children, yet real wages continue to stagnate or fall, then few options remain for maintaining their standard of living.[14] As the Republican governor of Indiana, Robert D. Orr, put it in an address to the state legislature:

> We are a nation under economic attack and unprepared for the rigors of international competition. If we do not do something now to become competitive, the next generation will become the first in fifteen generations of Americans to inherit a standard of living lower than that of their parents.[15]

Looking back, there is little wonder that, given the lack of growth in productivity and real income, many job-training programs were able to produce only modest increases in earnings or that the poverty rate stopped falling as it had, from 22 percent in 1959 to 11 percent in 1973. In fact, after 1973 the poverty rate began to increase, at first gradually and then more dramatically during the 1980 and 1982 recessions, reaching 15.2 percent by 1983 before falling back to 14.0 percent in 1984 and 13.6 percent by 1986.[16]

If overall productivity does not pick up significantly—and it has not, primarily because of lags in the service sector rather than in the manufacturing sector—real wages, and thus our standard of living, will fail to rise to any substantial degree, especially in the face of competition from low-wage countries. Given the preponderance of white-collar and service jobs in the service industries, improvements in productivity will have to be generated largely by more efficiency in these occupations. As Lester Thurow, dean of the Sloan School of Management, has noted:

> To get American productivity growing again white-collar workers and service workers are going to have to be at the forefront of the productivity

revolution. Getting them there is going to be a management and socio-logical challenge of the first magnitude.[17]

Schooling, Skills, and Earnings

Young workers, especially those with limited education, were hurt the most by this nearly fifteen-year period of real earnings stagnation. If we compare the real median incomes of five different age groups at two points in time, 1973 and 1984, we see that although all workers suffered some decline in earnings, younger workers experienced the greatest declines. Young male adults (ages twenty to twenty-four) in 1984 had real median incomes that were one-third less than young adults of the same age group eleven years earlier.* Because of their greater seniority, more mature male workers, who had more work experience and were less susceptible to declines in employment in goods-producing sectors, were better able to retain their real in-comes.[18] As a result, the older a group, the less its members suffered (see Table 1).

Table 1   Trends in real median incomes of males 20–64 years old in the United States, 1973–84, by age subgroup (in 1984 dollars)

Age Group	Real Median Income ($) 1973	1984	Percent Change 1973–84
20–24	12,052	8,046	− 33.2
25–34	23,576	18,093	− 23.3
35–44	28,114	24,566	− 12.6
45–54	27,275	24,589	− 9.8
55–64	22,323	19,527	− 12.5

Note: The median income data pertain only to those men with an income during each calendar year. The Consumer Price Index–All Urban Consumers (CPI–U) was used to convert 1973 incomes into 1984 dollar equivalents.
Source: U.S. Bureau of the Census, *Current Population Reports,* Series P-60, No. 97 and No. 151.

---

* To understand the dimensions of these problems, we focus on trends in male earnings patterns because they are not confounded by the radical changes in labor force participation that occurred among women in the 1970s.

As alarming as these numbers are, they understate the problem since they exclude young men with no reported incomes, and the proportion of young men, especially young black men, without incomes or earnings has grown significantly.[19] For example, in 1973 only 7.3 percent of all twenty- to twenty-four-year-old males reported no earnings; by 1984, 12 percent of all twenty- to twenty-four-year-olds had no earnings. This rise was not the result of college students failing to seek employment. Rather it was the failure of males with limited education to obtain any employment whatsoever. Among black dropouts in this same age group in 1973, only 14.2 percent reported no earnings, but by 1984 a whopping 43 percent reported no earnings.[20]

Educational attainment was a second key determinant of who suffered most from the wage stagnation of the 1970s and early 1980s. Again, although nearly all males were adversely affected, within each age group males with the least education experienced the largest declines in mean earnings. For example, a comparison of the real mean earnings of twenty- to twenty-four-year-old high school dropouts in 1973 with a similar cohort in 1984 shows that annual earnings declined by 41.6 percent, from $11,210 to $6,552, while earnings of high school graduates, those with some college, and those with a B.S. or B.A. degree declined by a smaller amount: 30.1 percent, 26.1 percent, and 11.0 percent, respectively (see Table 2). For those who worked, these declines in real earnings were the result of fewer hours and weeks of employment as well as lower hourly wages.

Although the real mean earnings of black dropouts and high school graduates declined nearly twice as much as those of whites or Hispanics, young black male college graduates raised their earnings by 16.3 percent during this period. Considering that white and Hispanic college graduates' earnings declined, this was a remarkable accomplishment. This finding of a sharp divergence between the mean incomes of college-educated black males and those of their less educated counterparts is not unique to the twenty- to twenty-four-year-old age group. It holds true for black males twenty-five to twenty-nine and thirty to thirty-four years old as well. William Julius Wilson, Martin Kilson, and others have noted that this growing inequality in the earnings of blacks with sharply different levels of education is contributing to the rise of two Americas among young black families, a black underclass and a black middle class.[21]

Table 2 Trends in the real mean annual earnings of 20- to 24-year-old males, 1973–84, by educational attainment and race/ethnic group (in 1984 dollars)

Level of Education	Real Mean Earnings ($) of All (20–24)		% Change in Earnings, 1973–84			
	1973	1984	All	White	Black	Hispanic
No diploma	11,210	6,552	− 41.6	− 38.7	− 61.3	− 38.6
H.S. graduate	14,342	10,020	− 30.1	− 26.1	− 52.2	− 28.1
Some college	12,386	9,153	− 26.1	− 22.0	− 50.3	− 31.6
College grad.	13,970	12,443	− 11.0	− 12.2	+ 16.3	− 14.9

Note: Earnings data pertain only to those twenty- to twenty-four-year-old males who did not cite "school" as their major activity at the time of the March 1974 and March 1985 surveys.
Source: March 1974 and March 1985 Current Population Survey public use tapes; calculations by Center for Labor Market Studies, Northeastern University.

In report after report, employers have confirmed the growing importance of education and literacy in the labor market.[22] These commission reports argue that to participate productively in today's economy, everyone must have a well-rounded high school education at a minimum. Employers' views should be taken seriously; they are practicing what they preach. More than ever before, the labor market is distinguishing between those with a high school diploma and those who left school before graduation. For eighteen- to twenty-four-year-old males, for example, the gap between the mean annual incomes of a high school dropout and a high school graduate was 31 percent in the early 1960s, but had risen to 59 percent in the early 1980s. The growing gap between the mean incomes of dropouts and graduates also holds for somewhat older workers, although for them work experience is a more immediate determinant of their earnings than the high school diploma (see Figure 2).

"Credential inflation" may explain some of the higher premium that employers placed on the diploma. The baby-boom surplus of young entry workers in the 1960s and 1970s allowed employers to raise their application requirements, even though the skills required for certain jobs might not have changed appreciably. But if credentialling accounted for the change, the baby-bust decline in the number of teenage

Figure 2 Percentage increment in mean annual incomes of high school graduates (no college) over high school dropouts, 18–34-year-old males, by age group, 1960–1984

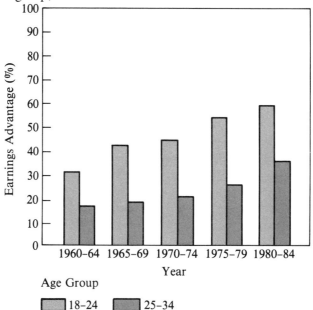

and young adult workers that began in 1979 coupled with the strong economic expansion that has been under way since 1982 should have resulted in a lowering of entrance requirements. But as we describe later, little evidence exists to confirm such a trend reversal.

Achievement data also provide evidence that employers value skills and knowledge. It is important to distinguish between achievement— what a person knows as measured by a standardized test—and attainment, the last grade completed in school. When employers hire, they do not have access to achievement scores, so they generally hire on the basis of attainment. Attainment often signals a capacity to "stick to it," a trait that employers value. As Table 3 shows, graduates with achievement scores in the second lowest quintile in a distribution of basic skills test scores earn slightly more than dropouts with scores in the second highest quintile, indicating that attainment is an important determinant of earnings. Ultimately, however, employers value both attainment and achievement. The data show that employers reward achievement with more work and more pay. Within each category—

Table 3   Average annual mean earnings, 1978–80, of those aged 20–23 in 1981, by sex, high school graduation status, and level of academic skills

Basic Academic Skills Level[a]	Males' Earnings ($)		Females' Earnings ($)	
	Dropouts	**Graduates**	**Dropouts**	**Graduates**
Lowest quintile	4,616	6,013	1,429	2,936
Second lowest quintile	6,595	8,639	2,156	4,235
Middle quintile	6,765	8,190	3,102	4,629
Second highest quintile	8,321	9,433	2,465	5,469
Highest quintile	9,086	10,738	4,146	6,003

[a] Based on the Armed Forces Qualification Test (AFQT). The AFQT test score distribution used in computing the above quintiles is that for all eighteen- to twenty-three-year-old non-enrolled high school graduates and high school dropouts as of the 1981 NLS (National Longitudinal Survey of Young Americans) interview. Only persons who completed twelve or fewer years of school by 1981 and who were not enrolled in school at the time of the 1979, 1980, and 1981 interviews are included in the analysis. (See Appendix A.)

Source: National Longitudinal Survey of Young Americans, 1979–81 public use tapes; tabulations by the Center for Labor Market Studies, Northeastern University.

high school graduates and high school dropouts—those with better skills earn more. This pattern holds regardless of race, sex, or family background (see Appendix C). Christopher Jencks and his colleagues reported similar findings when they examined a variety of studies on earnings, education, and family background to determine who gets ahead in America.[23] Controlling for the influence of other variables, they estimated, for example, that each one-point increase in test scores was associated with about a 1 percent increase in annual earnings. It is probably safe to assume that employers discern and reward better skills because they find that workers who know more also learn more quickly and are more productive than workers who know less.[24]

Occupations and Earnings
The national economy's transformation from a manufacturing to a service base has permanently affected the occupational mix and earnings structure of the labor market. The goods-producing sectors are dominated by blue-collar occupations (crafts, operative) while many finance and private service industries are dominated by white-collar

workers where a higher-than-average proportion of jobs are in professional, managerial, and administrative categories.

Throughout the 1970s the proportion of all jobs that were white-collar increased by about a tenth while the proportion of all jobs that were blue-collar declined by a similar amount. Meanwhile, jobs in retail trade and in the low-wage segment of the service sector increased by a couple of percentage points.[25] The back-to-back recessions of 1980 and 1982, the decline in full-time jobs as a proportion of all jobs, and the growth of low-wage jobs in the first half of the 1980s further exacerbated these shifts. Between 1979 and 1985, the U.S. economy generated a net of nearly 8.0 million new wage and salary jobs, even while losing more than 1.7 million jobs in the manufacturing sector.[26] But up to one-half of this job growth may have occurred in low-wage and part-time jobs in the retail trade and service sectors.[27] By comparison, only one-fifth of the new jobs created in the 1970s were of this kind.

The decline of the manufacturing sector as a major employer had a devastating impact on all young people, but its impact was especially severe for those with deficiencies in education and basic skills. Since early 1974 the proportion of young male workers employed in manufacturing industries has declined by one-fourth, while the proportion employed in the trade and service industries has increased by more than one-fifth. In early 1974 blue-collar craft, operative, and foreman jobs accounted for nearly half (46 percent) of the jobs held by employed black men, ages twenty to twenty-four. By 1984 these jobs accounted for about one-fourth (26.0 percent) of the jobs held by young black males.[28] It was this "silent firing" of young workers—those who were never hired to replace retiring workers—that is the big untold story underlying the decline of the manufacturing sector. These were frequently the jobs in which one could earn enough to support a family, even if one did not have a strong education.

Again, 1973 appears to have been a pivotal year. Before 1973 young people and especially minorities were gaining access to career manufacturing jobs, but after 1973, as the number of net new hires in these sectors declined, the next generation of young workers failed to gain entry to a similar degree. Thus, the pre-1973 period was characterized by sustained real earnings growth for all young people, but the post-1973 era saw these gains fading away. For example, from 1959 to 1973 the real median income of black males who were twenty

Table 4 Trends in the real median incomes of
20–24-year-old males with incomes, by race, U.S.:
1959, 1973, 1984 (in 1984 dollars)

Year	Income ($)		
	All Males	**White Males**	**Black Males**[a]
1959	9,165	9,635	6,172
1973	12,049	12,360	10,369
1984	8,036	8,378	5,768
	Percent Change		
1959–73	+31.5	+28.3	+68.0
1973–84	−33.3	−32.2	−44.4

[a] Data for 1959 are for all non-white males.
Source: U.S. Bureau of the Census, *Current Population Reports,*
Series P-60, selected years. The CPI–U index was used to convert
1959 and 1973 incomes into 1984 dollars.

to twenty-four years old increased by 68 percent; however, from 1973
to 1984 it fell by 44 percent (see Table 4). Young white men experienced similar but less dramatic swings in their real median incomes,
up by 28 percent from 1959 to 1973 and down by 32 percent from
1973 to 1984.

Earnings and Marriage

As each new group of young male workers entering the labor market
earned lower mean real wages and worked fewer hours annually during
the past decade, the percentage of young men with incomes sufficient
to support themselves and other potential family members with a standard of living above the poverty line also declined. In the early 1970s
nearly 60 percent of the young men who were twenty to twenty-four
years old were able to earn enough to support a family of three above
the poverty line; by 1984 only 42 percent could do so (see Table 5
and Figure 3).

The post-1973 period was especially damaging for minority youth.
In 1973 more than half (55 percent) of all twenty- to twenty-four-year-
old black males had earnings adequate to support a family of three
above the poverty line. By 1984 less than one-quarter, 23 percent, had
such earnings. The experience of Hispanic men was similar. Sixty-
one percent were able to support a family of three above the poverty

Table 5 Percent of 20–24-year-old males, all educational groups, with annual earnings at or above the three-person poverty line, by race/ethnic group, U.S.: 1973, 1979, 1984

Race/Ethnic Group	1973	1979	1984
All Males	59.4	57.3	41.7
White, non-Hispanic	60.4	60.3	46.0
Black, non-Hispanic	55.2	40.7	23.3
Hispanic	61.1	54.0	34.6

Source: U.S. Bureau of the Census, *Current Population Survey* public use tapes, March 1974, March 1980, and March 1985, tabulations by Center for Labor Market Studies, Northeastern University.

Figure 3 Percent of 20–24-year-old males with annual earnings at or above the three-person poverty line, by race/ethnic group, 1973, 1979, and 1984

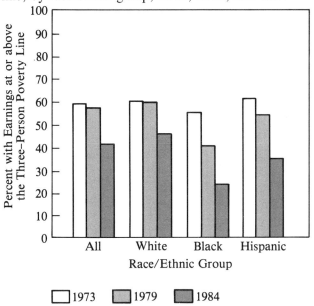

line in 1973 versus only 35 percent a decade later. One final, poignant point about the mean annual earnings of twenty- to twenty-four-year-old males without a diploma: with mean annual earnings of only $6,552 in 1984, the average male high school dropout could hardly have been expected to support a family. This was far less true in 1973, when high school dropouts had mean earnings above $11,000 (as was shown in Table 2).

The decline in the real earnings of young males has, in turn, had significant effects on their marriage behavior and family-formation patterns. Between 1964 and 1974 marriage rates among twenty- to twenty-four-year-old males declined by less than 3 percent (see Table 6 and Figure 4). During the next decade, however, there was a sudden acceleration of that decline. The proportion of young males who were married and living with their spouses declined by almost one-half, falling from 39.1 percent to 21.8 percent. Once again, black men were hit the hardest. For example, in 1974 nearly 30 percent of black men twenty to twenty-four were married and living with their spouses. By 1984 only 9 percent of such men were married. That represents a 70 percent decline in young black men's marriage rates.

Table 6   Percent of 20–24-year-old men who were married and living with their spouses, by race: selected years, 1964 to 1984

Year	All Races	White	Black
1964	41.6	42.3	37.6[a]
1969	42.3	43.7	32.7
1974	39.1	40.5	29.2
1979	28.8	30.4	18.4
1984	21.8	23.9	8.6

[a] The 1964 data are for all non-white males rather than black males only.

Source: U.S. Bureau of the Census, *Current Population Reports,* Series P-20.

We estimate that about one-half of the decline in marriage rates among high school dropouts and nearly 30 percent of the decline among high school graduates (no college) was due to the decline in their earnings. In fact, if the 1973 earnings distribution for male high school dropouts had prevailed in 1984, marriage rates would have been almost one-third higher among whites and nearly 82 percent higher among blacks.[29] Among school dropouts and high school graduates not going on to college, earnings and marriage patterns move almost in tandem.

Figure 4   Percent of white and black males, 20–24
years old, married and living with spouse, U.S.:
1964–1984

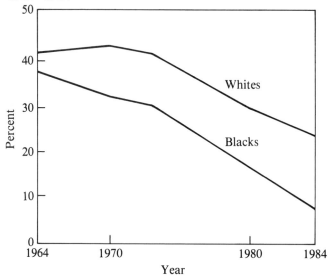

Source: U.S. Bureau of the Census. *Current Population Reports*
(Selected Years).

Young men who have earnings above the three-person family poverty
line are typically 2.5 to 3.0 times more likely to be married than their
counterparts with below poverty earnings.

Without adequate earnings, men are far less likely to marry, and
women are less likely to marry men who cannot support them, even
when they are the fathers of their children. The birth rates of teens
and women twenty to twenty-four years old are not rising. In fact,
overall birth rates among teens and young female adults have been
declining since 1960. It is the *share* of all births to young women that
occur out of wedlock that has risen since the 1960s, and not so co-
incidentally, the greatest surge occurred in the last fifteen years.[30]

Many people believe that this increase in out-of-wedlock births as
a proportion of all births is a sign of declining morals among youth.
Yet contrary to popular wisdom, the rate of out-of-wedlock childbearing among all single women has stayed about the same in the past
decade and has declined for blacks. Because there are more unmarried
women and since childbearing among married women has declined, a

steady rate of out-of-wedlock childbearing among this larger pool of single women meant that their children would constitute a higher proportion of all children born to women in this age group. In sum, the out-of-wedlock childbearing rate has remained stable, but births to unmarried women now account for a larger share of all births because younger married women are having fewer children and because there are more single women (see Figures 5a and 5b).

Obviously, economic change that affects the real earnings of males is not the only force at work here. Other forces influence marriage and family patterns. Divorce rates have been on the rise since the 1950s, and divorce remains the prevalent route to female-headed households, especially for whites. In the minority community, female-headed households have been a concern since the time of W.E.B. Dubois, and both male and female blacks, especially those who are less educated, are increasingly unlikely to marry at all.[31] Young people have also been delaying marriage to go to college. Finally, the baby boom placed a strain on the labor market's absorptive capacities during the 1970s. (It should be noted, however, that most of the deterioration in the labor-market position of young men occurred after 1979, when the size of that group was actually shrinking.)

To sum up: It is clear that the wage stagnation of the 1970s and the recession-induced unemployment and underemployment of the 1980s severely affected the earning capacity of young men, especially those with limited education and skills. These changes dealt a devastating blow to family-formation patterns, which in turn helped to increase the number of children living in poverty. For example, in March 1974 approximately one-fourth of all children in families headed by twenty- to twenty-four-year-olds were poor, but by March 1985 nearly half of the children living in such young households were poor. More than 12 million American children live in poverty today, and one in every five newborn children begins life in a poor household.[32]

Among children, the likelihood of being raised in poverty is inextricably bound up with family structure. Longitudinal data indicate that practically all children who grow up in a female-headed household (93 percent) can expect to spend at least part of their childhood in poverty while only one-fifth of those those who spend their entire childhood in stable two-parent families will be poor for any length of time. The most distressing point, however, is that two-thirds of the children who

Figure 5a   Number of live births per 1,000
women, by selected age group, U.S., 1960–1983

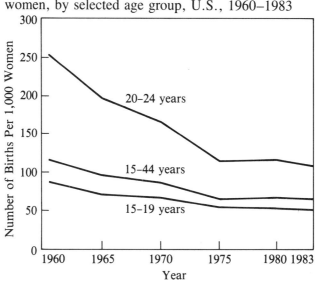

Figure 5b   Birth rates for married and for unmarried women, age 15–44, U.S., 1960–1982

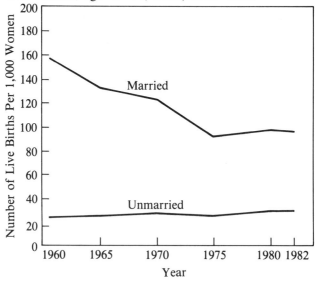

grow up entirely in single-parent households spend nearly their entire childhood in poverty as compared to only 2 percent of those who grow up in two-parent households.[33] Coming from a mother-only household and spending a major portion of one's childhood in poverty has severe consequences for children's future school performance and for their prospects for economic independence as adults.[34]

The key thing to remember, however, is that as a nation we cannot go back. Even if real earnings begin to grow again, two groups will be left behind: those with limited educational attainment and female heads of households. An above-average share of the new job growth over the remainder of the century will occur in the professional, technical, management, and administrative fields, and some rehiring may occur in the manufacturing and transportation sectors. For most of these jobs, good basic skills and, increasingly, post-high school education and training will be minimum requirements for hiring. The primary labor market is virtually shutting down for those with limited skills and attainment.

Single-parent households will have an especially difficult time, particularly when they are headed by women with limited formal education. Poverty among families headed by young women has been on the rise in the past decade. Eighty-five percent of all families headed by a twenty- to twenty-four-year-old female who dropped out of high school were poor in 1985. Only about half of all poor households headed by women have any wage earners, and most of those who are working are only able to work part time or part of the year because of family responsibilities. Thus, real wage growth alone will not easily lift these one-earner families above the poverty line. Nor is wage growth likely to result in a major upturn in marriage rates for this group of mothers as they age. Even worse, according to Levy, a resumption of real wage growth seems likely to widen the income gap between one-parent and two-parent households, since more than 60 percent of all young two-parent families now have two earners. As the wages of these two-earner households grow, the distance in income between the poor and the rest of the population will increase.[35]

The Achievement Gap Between U.S. and Foreign Students

Growth in the real wages of young workers is a necessary first step in solving these problems, but it will not come easily. It will depend on our ability to get productivity growing again, and we have been unable to accomplish this in the 1980s, particularly in the non-manufacturing sector of the economy.

Part of the difficulty lies in our growing global economic interdependence. Exports and imports comprise an ever larger share of U.S. economic activity. For most of the past two decades, our major international competitors have had faster rates of productivity growth and are rapidly catching up with our productivity levels. Lester Thurow and other economists argue that to have a world-class economy that can compete with the Europeans and the Japanese in the high value-added products and services that offer high wages, we will need to increase our savings rate and invest in scientific research and development, in new production techniques, and in the education and training of our work force.[36]

Thus, economists, businessmen, and others are very concerned about education and basic skills. Every recent international educational test has revealed a large gap between the performance of American children and the children of other industrialized countries. In a recent international comparison of mathematical proficiency conducted by the National Academy of Sciences, the performance of U.S. high school seniors ranked in the bottom 25th percentile, the lowest of all industrialized countries. Japanese students scored the highest. U.S. students performed the worst on questions concerning mathematical systems and patterns—the very skills that underlie the industries of the future: chemistry, engineering, mathematics, physics, biology, and computer sciences.[37]

The academic performance of American students is, however, related to effort, not simply to native ability. At present, American youth attend school only 180 days a year, while European and Japanese youth go to school 220 and 240 days per year, respectively. Approximately two-thirds of Japanese students do five hours or more of homework each week, while only one-quarter of American students do so.[38] Moreover, the average American student is absent nearly twenty days per year, while the average Japanese youth is absent only three days. Further, the Japanese student spends more hours in school each day than the American student, and 75 percent of Japanese students attend after-school private academies (Juku schools) to overcome educational deficiencies and get ahead of their peers. In his classic study of Japanese education, Thomas Rohlen estimates that by the time the average

Japanese youngster graduates from high school, he or she will have spent the equivalent of four more years in school than the average American.[39]

It should come as no surprise, then, that Japanese youth consistently out-perform American youth on standardized tests. In fact, the skills of the average Japanese high school graduate rival those of many American college graduates. According to Lester Thurow, all Japanese high school students take calculus, but only 10 percent of Americans do; only half of 1 percent of the Japanese are illiterate, compared with 10 to 13 percent of Americans; and, although more than 90 percent of all young Japanese graduate from high school, only about 80 to 85 percent of young Americans do. In Japan, 40 percent of all college graduates major in science and engineering; in America only 8 percent major in these fields.

Simplistic cross-country comparisons like these can be misinterpreted. As Merry White demonstrates, the Japanese culture celebrates children and education.[40] Teachers are revered, and Japanese mothers see the nurturing of their children's educational development as their primary life goal. The population is ethnically, linguistically, and, in a comparative sense, economically homogeneous. Everyone is assumed to have the ability to succeed, and failure is blamed on lack of effort. The result is a level of enthusiasm and a sense of purpose that would be difficult to duplicate.

Of course, there is also the familiar claim that Japanese education is too routinized and test-focused and thus stifles creativity. Based on his 1974 observations, Thomas Rohlen characterized Japanese instruction as "... a monochromatic and monotonous ... encyclopedic approach to learning."[41] The more recent observations of Merry White suggest that these negative attributes may be overstated. She concludes that the superior preparation of Japanese students has combined with their extraordinary enthusiasm for school to give the Japanese the lead in creativity as well.

These disagreements notwithstanding, the test results are difficult to argue with. In Japan, virtually everyone succeeds; there is relatively little variation in test performance among students. Because of global competition, it is unlikely that we will be able to ignore the new standards of educational performance and efficiency that the Japanese have set for the world.[42] This poses a fundamental dilemma for American education. We have celebrated individual choice and diversity in performance, content in the mythology that educational laggards would find other avenues in which to excel. Such an approach may have made sense in earlier days, when educational performance was not as directly tied to work opportunities and real earnings. We may no longer be able to afford such complacency.

Japanese educational techniques cannot and should not be emulated in all key respects. However, there can be little doubt about what is needed to improve American students' educational performance in the key subjects of mathematics, science, and engineering. According to recent findings of the ''High School and Beyond'' longitudinal survey, only 5.6 percent of all 1980 high school graduates in the United States who went on to college were majoring in biology, engineering, and the physical sciences by their junior year.[43] Who were these students? They were those with the highest tested academic skills in high school. In fact, students who scored in the top quartile of the High School and Beyond tests of reading, vocabulary, and mathematics were 108 times more likely than those who scored in the bottom quartile to major in these critical fields. Only .14 percent of those with bottom quartile skills majored in these fields.

Regrettably, the trend for some time has been away from making the necessary investments in our nation's economic future. Between 1940 and 1967 we added an average of 1.0 grade level to the median educational level of the nation's civilian work force every ten years. But in the 1967 to 1983 period, we added only one-half of a grade level.[44] Moreover, college enrollment rates among all young adults (eighteen to twenty-four) peaked in the late 1960s. Today a smaller proportion of young black adults is going to college than in the mid-1970s, even though their share of the population is rising. Minorities already account for one-half of the elementary and secondary public school populations in Texas and California and one-third in New York and Florida. Yet among eighteen- to twenty-four-year-old black high school graduates, college enrollment rates have declined from 34 percent in 1976 to 26 percent in 1985 and for Hispanics from 36 percent to 27 percent.[45] At the same time, job projections for the year 2000 indicate that new jobs will require a work force whose median level of education is 13.5 years (compared to 12.8 years now).[46]

The United States is being outdistanced in other areas as well. Although we are generally acknowledged to have one of the finest systems of higher education in the world, practically no attention is paid to the severe inadequacies of our vocational training and apprenticeship systems. We have the least well articulated system of school-to-work transition in the industrialized world. Japanese students move directly into extensive company-based training programs, and European students often participate in closely interconnected schooling and apprenticeship training programs. In fact, American visitors to European countries marvel at their commitment of national resources to youth. In Austria, Sweden, West Germany, and Switzerland, it is virtually impossible to leave school without moving into some form of apprenticeship or other vocational training.[47]

By contrast, American guidance and counseling are geared almost solely toward the needs of the college-bound. For example, High School and Beyond follow-up interviews with a representative sample of high school seniors from the class of 1980 revealed that only 5 percent of graduates were participating in an apprenticeship training program within the first year following graduation from high school, and only 1 percent of graduates reported being enrolled in an apprenticeship program three years after graduation from high school.[48] In sharp contrast, between 33 and 55 percent of all those who left school at ages sixteen to eighteen in such European nations as Austria, Germany, and Switzerland had entered apprenticeships in the late 1970s.[49] Students, employers, and postsecondary technical training programs in the United States find each other on a ''catch as catch can'' basis.

In summary, postsecondary education, training, and apprenticeship programs for all those who leave school, not just for the college-bound, are investments that we have failed to make, creating a growing number of school-to-work transition problems. Clearly, if the United States is going to have a competitive work force, we will have to close the achievement gap between ourselves and our major foreign competitors. This means that we must strengthen the quality and quantity of primary, secondary, and postsecondary education for all Americans.

Those Who Are Left Out

Alarm about the educational "tide of mediocrity" is at its heart a concern about the average achievement levels of our nation's citizens. Raising the scores of those at the bottom is the surest and most cost-effective way of raising the average and is likely to have favorable consequences for long-term income distribution. The Japanese have learned this lesson well. As James Fallows points out, they claim to "have the best bottom 50 percent in the world."[50]

Here in America, the numerical importance of those currently at the bottom will increase. Dramatic demographic changes already at work will decrease the total size of the young adult population (eighteen to twenty-four years old) by more than one-fourth between 1979 and 1995.[51] In addition, a higher share of this smaller total will be composed of minority and economically disadvantaged groups. Thus, those at the bottom of the distribution curve of skills and schooling will increasingly hold the key to the future of America's performance.

This is the second achievement gap—a domestic one between bottom-scorers and top-scorers, between minorities and non-minorities, and between the poor and the non-poor. Here we find the most immediate problems facing the American educational system. The data on these achievement gaps are sobering. Yet twenty-five recent major reports on American education have mentioned them only in passing. It is distressing that on virtually every major standardized test, minorities and the poor are concentrated in the bottom fifth of the test score distribution. This is true for the National Assessment of Educational Progress (NAEP) reading, writing, and mathematics tests for nine-, thirteen-, and seventeen-year-olds; the "High School and Beyond" longitudinal analysis of tenth and twelfth graders; a national sample of fourteen- to twenty-one-year-olds who were given the Armed

Forces Qualification Test (AFQT); the recent Educational Testing Service (ETS) assessment of the literacy proficiencies of the nation's young adults; and the Scholastic Aptitude Tests (SATs) and Graduate Record Examinations (GREs). On the average, black and Hispanic scores are about 70 percent of white scores, with a thirty-point gap on the NAEP, a 200-point gap on the SAT combined verbal and quantitative test, and a 300-point gap on the combined verbal and mathematics portions of the GRE. Although the gap has closed markedly over the past few years, it remains unacceptably large.[52]

These disparities in reading and mathematics scores have a number of dire consequences. In conjunction with other factors, these tests—the AFQT, the SAT, and the GRE—are reasonably good predictors of who will enter and complete the army, college, and graduate school.[53] There is also a strong relationship between achievement and future employment, job performance, and earnings.[54] According to the *New York Times,* in a recent testing of New York City high school graduates by the New York Telephone Company, 84 percent of the job applicants failed to pass its entry test for telephone repair trainees and operators. A consortium of New York City banks made a commitment to hire 300 high school graduates from five inner-city schools, but found that only 100 students were able to meet entry requirements that included an eighth-grade test of reading comprehension and mathematics skills. This performance gap deserves to be the central focus of local, state, and federal educational efforts throughout the remainder of this century.

Consider, for example, the issue of joblessness among black youth. Researcher after researcher has examined this problem and concluded that we simply cannot explain why the unemployment rate of black teenagers remains so high and why their employment/population ratios (the proportion of all youths who are employed) remain so far below those of other groups.[55] Popular explanations from the 1970s are increasingly irrelevant: lower levels of educational attainment, the federal minimum wage, competition from baby-boom peers and adult women, and the effects of recession. High school completion rates among young blacks have increased over the past decade. The total size of the youth population has declined by 13 percent in the past five years. The real value of the federal minimum wage has declined considerably. At least in terms of net overall job creation, the national economy is booming. Yet black youth unemployment statistics remain at very high levels.

Because young black high school graduates often fare worse in the labor market than white high school dropouts, some have concluded that discrimination is the primary culprit. Other researchers point out that black youth who go to church and do not live in public housing are more likely to find jobs.[56]

One major explanation that is rarely offered is that of the literacy proficiencies and achievement scores of young blacks. The average black seventeen-year-old reads at the same level as a white thirteen-year-old. How well can we expect inner-city blacks to fare when they must compete in the labor market against their white and black peers who were educated in suburban high schools? The fact is that the average black high school graduate scores below white high school dropouts on the armed services' basic skills test (AFQT) of reading, vocabulary, and mathematics.[57] American rhetoric continues its slogans about education as the great equalizer. But so long as severe race and class segregation continues to characterize living patterns, inequities will persist in American schooling, from lower expectations for student performance to unequal school finances.

To sum up, the events that precipitated this story began in 1973 and were largely macroeconomic in nature. It is clear that economic, occupational, and demographic changes have heightened the importance of basic skills. Moreover, skills and economic growth are interdependent. Without adequate growth, there will not be enough jobs for those with limited skills; however, a less skilled work force will impede economic growth and improvements in productivity. Furthermore, even if the economic pie grows more rapidly, the consequences for those with limited education and skills will be dire enough to constitute an argument for action.

Three Problems That Confound

There are also a number of non-economic reasons to be concerned about low levels of basic skills. Like a two-edged sword, they mark economic victims and, at the same time, they help perpetuate some of our most perplexing social problems—including poverty, high school dropouts, teenage pregnancy, crime, and youth joblessness and underemployment. City, state, and federal legislators are currently grappling with the design of dropout-prevention programs, the formulation of teenage pregnancy policies, and the redesign of the nation's youth

training and welfare systems. But few of the proposed legislative responses reflect the interrelationship of these problems, the basic skills
crisis, and economic and demographic changes.

Too often we have been treating symptoms rather than causes.
Teenage parenting, youth joblessness, and dropping out of school are
closely intertwined. Yet the researchers and practitioners who work
on these issues generally view them as distinct problems. Sociologists
and social workers focus on the family and teenage pregnancy, educators concentrate on schooling and dropouts, and labor economists
emphasize employment and training. This has led to a circle of endless
"mysteries" and "puzzles" that have some of the finest researchers
and leaders in the country concluding that we simply do not know
what to do about these problems. For example, some sociologists have
concluded that the teen-parenting problem has its roots in the youth
unemployment problem, while youth employment experts point to the
lack of a diploma as a major factor in youth unemployment. Meanwhile, those who study school dropouts blame this problem on students'
lack of self-confidence and self-esteem, teen pregnancy, the lack of
job opportunities, and schools' indifference.[58]

Between 1978 and 1980 we provided 76,000 jobs in the federal
Youth Incentive Entitlement Pilot Projects in the belief that part-time
jobs could keep young people in school. We have provided sex education, believing that knowledge about contraception and about the
consequences of teenage childbearing would reduce the number of
unwanted pregnancies. Special counseling programs have been initiated to respond to the complicated needs of dropouts so that they would
know that someone cares.[59] However, although jobs helped those
who apparently would have stayed in school anyway to earn more
both during high school and when they graduated, they did not keep
dropout-prone youth in school.[60] Similarly, even though contraceptive
knowledge is necessary if unwanted pregnancies are to be avoided,
knowledge by itself has seldom altered behavior.[61] In each case, we
helped those on the margins but seldom those at the core, those suf-
fering from multiple problems.

Few people realize the critical role that basic skills deficiencies
play in each of these stubborn social problems. The National Longitudinal Survey of Youth Labor Market Experience contains data on a
representative national sample of youth who were fourteen to twenty-

one years of age when they were first interviewed and who have been re-interviewed annually from 1979 to 1986. Some 11,900 sample members were given the Armed Forces Qualification Test, a straightforward test of reading, word knowledge, and basic mathematics, which the military uses to determine whether young people have the necessary skills to enter the armed services (see Appendix A). The AFQT is generally regarded as one of the least culturally biased of tests, and a substantial number of minority applicants have obtained passing scores.

Yet its results show an alarming, direct relationship between basic skill levels and all three of the social problems enumerated above. Those with limited reading, mathematics, and vocabulary skills are much more likely to experience some social pathology. The lower the test score, the higher the concentration of people experiencing a particular social problem. Nearly half, 46 percent, of all young people aged nineteen to twenty-three who are poor rank in the lowest fifth of the test score distribution. The findings of the more recent national literacy testing of young adults by the Educational Testing Service are similar.[62] Of those with special problems—the jobless, dropouts, welfare dependents, or unwed parents—between 40 and 59 percent score in the lowest fifth of the test (see Table 7). The average unwed parent is at the 21st percentile. By comparison, the military's minimum cut-off point for training is the 30th percentile, and most of those who enter the armed services score significantly above that level.

Achievement (basic skills) determines attainment (number of years of schooling completed), which then determines employability and earnings, which influences the likelihood of marrying and bearing children within a two-parent family. Thus, there is a strong relationship between low basic skills and the incidence of welfare dependency (see Figure 6) among young adults.[63] It is also clear that the higher the test score in reading, word knowledge, and mathematics, the less likely it is that a young person will drop out of school prior to graduation (see Figure 7).

This relationship between skills and school completion is dramatic (see Figure 8 and, for further examples, Appendix B). A startling one-half of all 1979 high school juniors who scored in the bottom fifth of the AFQT test distribution for sixteen- to seventeen-year-olds had failed to graduate by 1981. Only 4 percent of those with scores in the top fifth failed to graduate. If we want to reach the lowest-scoring dropouts

Table 7 AFQT test score position of 19–23-year-olds by poverty and social/economic problem group, United States: 1981

Socioeconomic Characteristic	Percent in Lowest Fifth of Basic Skills	Percent Below-Average Basic Skills
Poor	46	77
One or more social/ economic problems	41	75
Jobless	40	72
Dropout	52	85
Public assistance recipient	53	79
Unwed parent	59	85
Arrested in past year	37	68
—— **Mean Percentile Ranking in Basic Skills Distribution** ——		
All 19- to 23-year-olds		50
Arrested		32
Jobless		26
Dependent		24
Poor		23
Two social problems		22
Poor plus one social problem		21
Unwed parent		21
Dropout		20
Poor and idle		18
Poor and dependent		16
Three or more social problems		15

Source: National Longitudinal Surveys of Youth Labor Market Experiences, 1979 to 1981; tabulations by Center for Labor Market Studies, Northeastern University.

who constitute the core of the dropout problem, we must address the syndrome that is the major cause of their leaving school: low achievement, falling behind modal grade, poor school performance, and a sense that they cannot catch up to their peers.[64] Any dropout-prevention program that does not focus on raising the academic achievement levels of students is unlikely to have a significant, lasting effect on school dropout rates or on the longer-term issues of employability and earnings.

Statistics relating basic skills proficiencies to the likelihood of be-

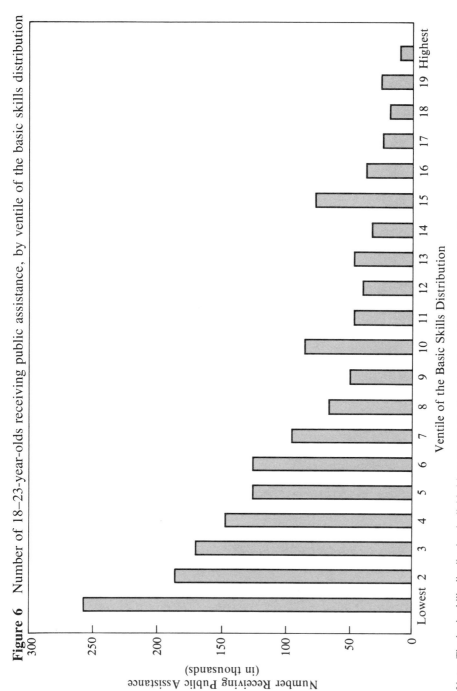

Figure 6 Number of 18–23-year-olds receiving public assistance, by ventile of the basic skills distribution

Note: The basic skills distribution is divided into twenty equal parts with ventile one representing the bottom 5 percent and ventile 20 representing the top 5 percent of scores (See Appendix A). Looking at the lowest ventile, approximately 257,000 of the 1.0 million 18- to 23-year-olds with scores in the lowest 5 percent of the basic skills distribution are receiving public assistance. As one moves from the lowest to the highest ventile the proportion of people in each ventile receiving public assistance declines.

Figure 7   Number of 18–23-year-old high school dropouts, by ventile of the basic skills distribution

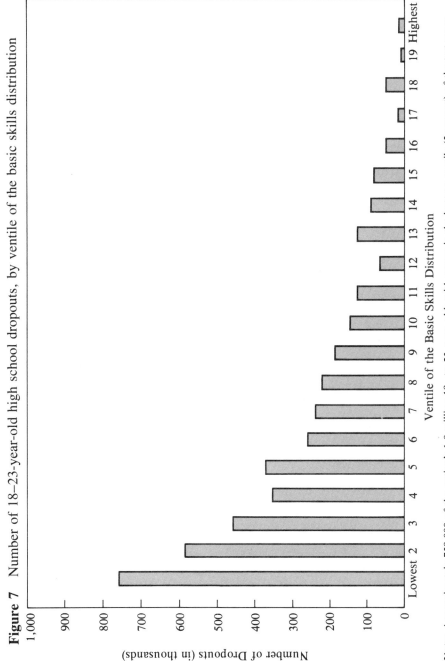

Note: Approximately 758,000 of the nation's 1.0 million 18– to 23–year-olds with scores in the bottom ventile (5 percent) of the test score distribution dropped out of school, as compared to 582,000 in ventile 2, 458,000 in ventile 3, and so forth.

Figure 8a Dropout rate by 1981, students aged
14–15 in 1979

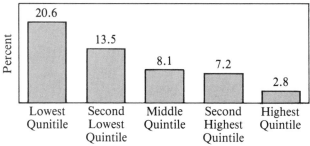

Note: One-fifth of 14- to 15-year-olds with scores in the bottom
fifth of a basic skills test had dropped out of school two years later, as
compared to only 3 percent of those with the highest scores.

Figure 8b Percent not graduating by 1981, students aged 16–17 in 1979 with ten years schooling

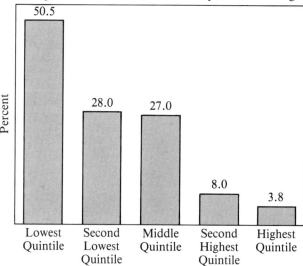

Note: One-half of all 16- to 17-year-olds with scores in the bottom
fifth of the distribution failed to graduate school on time. But a
quarter of those with average skills also failed to graduate.

Figure 9 Total number of out-of-wedlock births to women aged 19–23, by ventile of the basic skills distribution

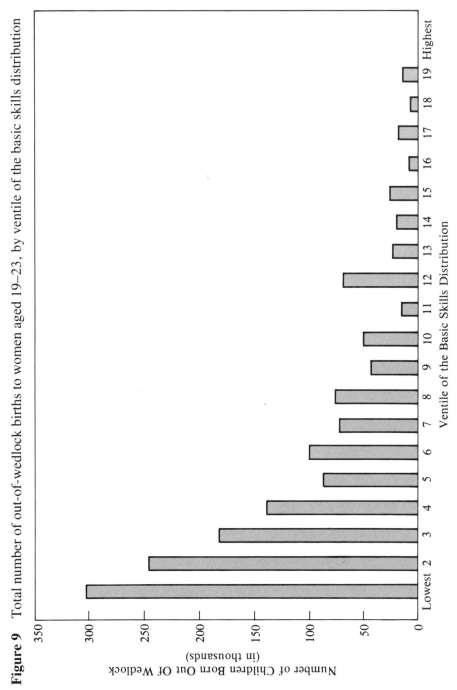

Note: Approximately 302,000 children were born to women aged 19 to 23 who had skills in the bottom of the test score distribution. As skill levels increase, the number of out-of-wedlock births that occur among women in each ventile decreases.

coming an unwed mother are even more alarming. The overwhelming majority of children born to all nineteen- to twenty-three-year-old women in America are born to mothers with the lowest basic skills. Nearly 60 percent of the total number of out-of-wedlock births that occurred among women nineteen to twenty-three years old occurred among those who scored in the lowest 20 percent on a basic skills test (see Figure 9). Given the extraordinary importance of the mother's education and skills level in determining the life options of her children, this is a matter of utmost concern.

Two questions remain. First, is it the relative position of young people in the basic skills distribution that determines the higher incidence of antisocial behavior and economic problems or is it their absolute skill level? The answer is probably both. The gaps in education, employment, and earnings between those with strong and weak literacy proficiencies are so large that it is difficult to imagine young people with low basic skills perceiving their futures as full of opportunity. As Kristen Moore has shown, a limited perception of future life options makes becoming a school dropout or a teenage parent an acceptable choice.[65] Individuals with AFQT test scores that fall in the bottom fifth of the national skills distribution have less than a sixth-grade reading ability. By comparison, individuals with scores in the top fifth of the AFQT test have approximately a twelfth-grade reading ability. Appendix B provides examples of the kinds of reading and mathematics tasks young people with these skills can complete. If these educational and related earnings gaps were narrower, the incidence of these social and economic problems would likely diminish, although those at the bottom would still evidence more of this behavior than those at the top of the skills distribution.

When we construct a profile of young people with identical characteristics, varying only their tested academic skill levels, the probability of various types of antisocial behavior decreases as skills increase. Take, for example, two girls, both from minority groups, raised in poor families by single parents, from inner-city areas, who have completed the same number of years of school. If one has better skills than the other, the one with the skills is likely to have higher earnings and less likely to be welfare dependent, pregnant, or criminally involved (see Tables 3 and 8, and Figures 6 and 7). A similar comparison of two non-minority children from two-parent families with middle-class incomes would produce a similar result. This is not to say, as Horace Mann did, that having good basic skills and more schooling would equalize the opportunities of poor and middle-class children.[66] It would not. The children with strong skills from a single-parent, poor household would still have a higher probability of early pregnancy and welfare dependency than the child with weak skills from a two-parent, middle-class family. However, the difference between the two would have narrowed significantly.

The second question is whether low basic skills are a cause of these other social problems, or whether they are a symptom of other underlying factors such as poverty. As E.C. Bentley noted in his classic mystery story, *Trent's Last Case,* "Between what matters and what seems to matter, how should the world we know judge wisely?" Causality in the social sciences is difficult to prove, since factors like skills, schooling, and poverty are interrelated. As we have seen in the preceding figures and tables, simple relationships between test scores and an array of socioeconomic problems reveal that, as compared to young people with above-average basic skills, those with low basic skills (the bottom 20 percent) were nine times more likely to have dropped out of school prior to graduation, eight times more likely to have become mothers out of wedlock, and four times more likely to become welfare dependent. These relationships hold for all sex, race, and income groups.

More to the point, when other factors are controlled for, basic skill levels are an independent determinant of earnings and antisocial behavior (see Appendix C and the estimates contained in Table 8). This factor alone accounts for about half of the explained variation in earnings patterns of young men and women. As test scores increase, earnings increase.[67]

Two Factors: Mother's Education and Summer Vacations

Clearly, low basic skills are an important underlying factor in many of our nation's most pressing social problems. Why do some young people acquire skills while others do not? First, as trite as it may sound, it is essential to remember that everything causes everything else in the generation-to-generation life cycle. Family background variables—such as family income, the neighborhoods children live in, whether there are two parents present, and most important of all, the mother's level of educational attainment—are crucial determinants of the life chances of children.[68]

The children of disadvantaged parents begin life behind their more advantaged counterparts. Since schooling is cumulative, children who begin behind stay behind, so that the best predictor of where a child will be in the second grade is where he or she was in the first grade, and so on. From the outset, disadvantaged children are limited by language and problem-solving skills they learn from their often poorly educated parents. As Thomas Sticht, Catherine Snow, and others have shown, parents with limited vocabularies are unlikely to promote extensive vocabulary development in their children.[69] Language development and the linguistic skills it symbolizes are a reliable predictor of cognitive ability. Parents who speak with their children, rather than at or past them, foster larger vocabularies and better language skills, and the development of reading and writing skills depends on those early language skills. Moreover, early language inadequacies appear to impair overall intellectual development, social skills, and psychological development.[70]

The intergenerational transmission of low basic skills promises to perpetuate the social problems described above in ways that will be detrimental to future economic growth and to efforts to reduce poverty. For example, Larry Bumpass and Sara McLanahan found that living in a mother-only family increased the odds of dropping out of school by more than 122 percent among whites and by 30 to 55 percent among blacks and Hispanics.[71] Somewhat surprisingly, however, having a mother who completed high school was a significantly more important determinant of the school enrollment of sixteen- to seventeen-year-old youth than whether the mother was married or whether she had an additional $10,000 in family income per year, although both of these factors were also important. Similarly, Andrew Sum and Robert Taggart recently used data from the National Longitudinal Survey of Youth Labor Market Experience to predict young people's test scores on the basis of their mothers' and fathers' education and other variables.[72] They found that an extra grade of attainment for the mother—when father's education, race, and region of the nation were constant—was associated with an extra half-grade equivalent of achievement for her children.[73] Because of this intergenerational effect of the parent's education on the child's, it is unlikely that we will be able to make a major difference for the child unless we place equal priority on education and academic remediation for the parent.

The problems of young people who have basic skills deficits are exacerbated during the summer when young people are not in school. For disadvantaged youth, the summer loss in learning is a critical factor in their long-term performance. In fact, Barbara Heyns and others who have looked at more than 3,000 Atlanta school children and more than 20,000 Title I participants during two school years and the intervening

Figure 10   Summer loss in learning

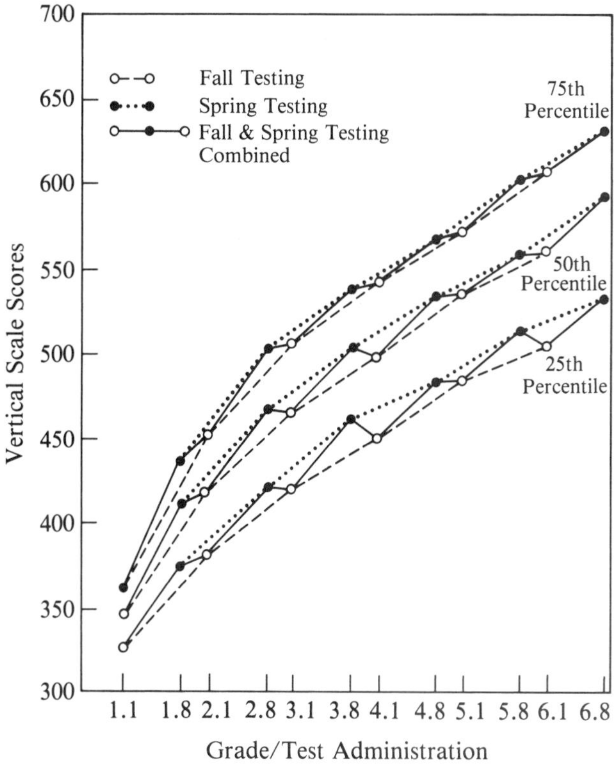

Note: The intervals 1.8 to 2.1, 2.8 to 3.1, and so forth correspond to the summer break from school. The zigzag lines show the summer loss that occurs among youth with test scores falling in the 25th, 50th, and 75th percentiles. Note that the largest loss occurs among those children who score in the lowest percentile, those who are already the farthest behind academically.

Source: Barbara Heyns, "Schooling and Cognitive Development: Is There a Season for Learning?" *Child Development* 58, no. 5 (1987), drawn from Leonard Syl Klisanoff, Sue Haggart, *Report No. 8: Summer Growth and the Effectiveness of Summer School,* report prepared for the Dept. of Education, RMC Research Corporation, Mountain View, California, February 1981.

summers, estimate that 80 percent of the difference between advantaged and disadvantaged children in year-to-year learning occurs during the summer.[74]

When school is in session, advantaged and disadvantaged children learn at about the same rate. But during the summer months when schools are closed, home and peer influences reassert themselves. At the end of the summer, advantaged children actually score higher on a standardized test than they did when the summer started while disadvantaged children fall further behind (see Figure 10). In advantaged homes, children are more likely to read and be read to, and they are more likely to go to places of educational interest. Disadvantaged children watch more television and are less likely to use standard English, a particular problem for children in non-English-speaking households.

The implications of these findings are far-reaching. The evidence suggests that many disadvantaged young people do learn when schools are in session.[75] By the same token, it is becoming clear that schools by themselves cannot solve the problem. Another obvious implication is the need to think long and hard about the agrarian origins of the current school year and the need for greater parental involvement in the education of children. Year-round schooling would place all youth on a more equal footing, since both advantaged and disadvantaged youth appear to learn at about the same rate during the school year.

Opportunities

On the basis of this evidence about the importance of the mother and the influence of family and peers during the summer, some analysts have concluded that socioeconomic status and family background pre-determine a situation that cannot be altered. The truth is otherwise: it is never too late to intervene. However, to make a meaningful difference, we must begin thinking about a lifetime of multiple interventions in which both mother's and child's skills are improved at key points in the development process.

For example, a team of researchers led by Frank Furstenberg followed 300 inner-city teenage mothers for seventeen years.[76] Most of the women were members of minority groups. Contrary to expectations, teenage childbearing did not lead inexorably to a lifetime of poverty and dependence for all the women. More than half eventually escaped poverty altogether. Education was the most potent avenue for escape from poverty and welfare, even when a mother waited until her twenties or thirties to go back to school. Mothers who returned to school were more likely to marry and more likely to work. This change in the mother's own life generally resulted in measurable improvements in the achievements of her children.

Furstenberg and his coauthors summarized their views on the development of these women in the following way:

> In brief, there are life courses characterized by welfare dependency, non-marriage, low education, and high fertility. Those whose life course takes such a trajectory are likely to remain on this path. But if they can escape, if they can alter this trajectory by getting a stable job, entering a stable marriage, acquiring educational credentials, or curtailing subsequent fertility, they are no more likely than others to fall back within this trajectory. Moreover, children benefit as their mother's life situation improves.[77]

These findings make it clear that we can help children by helping their mothers. Head Start for children plus Job Corps–type education and parenting instruction for mothers are likely to produce larger gains than either intervention alone. Turning schools into community education facilities that remain open to young adults late in the evenings and on weekends might be another way to help both parents and children. Rarely will a single intervention at a single point in time make a major difference. To overcome the forces that constrict the life options of young people growing up in poverty, interventions are needed all along the development continuum.

Yet questions remain. What effect would better basic skills and attainment have on young adult employment, earnings, school dropout rates, teenage pregnancy, and welfare dependency? We can attempt to estimate the effects of basic skills independent of other influences by using data from the National Longitudinal Surveys of Youth Labor Market Experience and multivariate statistical techniques to calculate the influence of each factor separately: additional years of attainment, the diploma, and achievement. Our estimates—which include statistical controls for such factors as standard demographic characteristics, health, socioeconomic background, geography, and local labor market conditions—suggest that completing an extra year of school at the secondary level would add $715 to the mean annual earnings ($5,105) of our sample of young men and women during the 1978–1980 period (see Table 8).[78] Obtaining a high school diploma would increase expected annual earnings by an additional $927, an effect equivalent to approximately 18 percent of the mean earnings level.[79] Each additional grade-level equivalent of tested basic skills, as measured by the AFQT test score, would increase expected annual earnings by $185, or 3.6 percent.[80]

Additional years of secondary schooling, the diploma, and higher basic academic skills also tend to reduce significantly the probability of dependency on public assistance, of out-of-wedlock births, and of criminal arrest (see Table 8). Each additional year of secondary schooling reduces the probability of public-assistance dependency by three percentage points, and possessing a high school diploma reduces the likelihood of public-assistance dependency by .7 percentage points, or approximately 8.2 percent.[81] Among unmarried women who were eighteen to twenty-one years old in 1979, the probability of giving birth to a child out of wedlock during the two years that followed was

Table 8   The estimated independent effects of increased skills or education on earnings, dependency, out-of-wedlock births, and arrests

Skills or Educational Factor	Regression-Estimated Annual Earnings Payoff[a]	
	Dollars	Percent
One grade more attainment[b]	715	14.0
High school diploma	927	18.2
Grade-equivalent of basic skills	185	3.6

Regression-Estimated Effects	Estimated Independent Effect	
	Probability in Percentage Points	Percent Change
Probability of dependency (18–22)	.0855	
One grade more attainment	−.0300	−35.1
Diploma net of attainment	−.0070	−8.2
One grade basic skills net of attainment and diploma	−.0046	−5.3
Probability of out-of-wedlock birth (18–21)	.0780	
One grade more attainment	−.0000	
Diploma net of attainment	−.0420	−53.8
One grade basic skills net of attainment and diploma	−.0050	−6.5
Probability of arrest (males, 18–23)	.0770	
One grade more attainment	−.0000	
Diploma net of attainment	−.0720	−93.5
One grade basic skills net of attainment and diploma	−.0048	−6.2

[a] See Appendix C for discussion of the characteristics of the reference group.

[b] Each factor—completing an additional year of school, obtaining a high school diploma, and testing a grade equivalent higher on a basic skills test—is calculated independently of the others. So, for example, the increase in earnings due to having a diploma does not include the effect of having completed another year of school.

7.8 percent. This probability was 4.2 percentage points lower for those who possessed a high school diploma. Each additional grade level of basic skills reduced the probability of out-of-wedlock childbearing by .5 percentage points. Finally, among males in 1980 who were eighteen to twenty-three-years old and not in a penal or similar institution, 7.7

percent reported having been arrested for a crime other than a minor traffic offense in the previous two years.[82] The probability of an arrest among males with a high school diploma was 7.2 percentage points lower. Each additional grade level of basic skills reduced the probability of an arrest by .5 percentage points.

On a more modest scale, our estimates suggest that if we could raise the mean tested basic skills of our nation's young adults by one grade equivalent, lifetime earnings would increase by 3.6 percent, and the likelihood of births out of wedlock, welfare dependency, and arrests would decline by 6.5 percent, 5.3 percent, and 6.2 percent, respectively. Even these small changes in tested basic skills would increase the nation's tax revenues and reduce transfer payments and other social costs associated with crime, dependency, and childbearing out of wedlock. Thus any investment in basic skills that succeeds in raising the average test scores of participants by a grade level should be extraordinarily cost effective. If these improvements in basic skills occurred at an earlier time—say, at age fourteen—the benefits would multiply, because better skills would yield more completed years of school and more high school and college graduations.[83]

Programs That Work

Although we believe these estimates of the effects of schooling and skills are conservative, they are also admittedly hypothetical. To note that young adults with better basic skills earn more does not ensure that these gains would actually accrue to disadvantaged youth with low skills who subsequently participated in a second-chance remedial education program. Can a special intervention effort raise the test scores of a disadvantaged child, youth, or adult by a grade or two? Would that gain actually result in higher earnings and less antisocial behavior?

Evidence is accumulating that disadvantaged children can learn and that their learning does lead to more educational attainment, graduations, and employment, and to lower rates of teenage childbearing and dependency. Special intervention programs facilitate that learning.

Preschool Education

Children who participated in the high-quality Perry Preschool program, for example, have achievement scores on standardized tests that are about one grade equivalent higher than the scores of randomly assigned control groups of children who did not participate in a preschool program.[84] Unlike IQ scores, these achievement scores are sustained, and even expand somewhat as children grow older. When these preschool program participants arrived in the first grade, they were perceived by their peers, parents, and teachers to be better prepared. During their teenage and young adult years, they were more likely to complete additional years of school, obtain a diploma, find a job, earn more, and go on to college. They were less likely to be classified as mentally retarded, become teenage parents, drop out of school, commit a crime, or be unemployed. In short, this $5,000 investment at age three or four produced lifetime benefits estimated at nearly $29,000 in earnings, taxes, and reduced social costs.[85]

Title I of the Elementary and Secondary Education Act

The "Sustained Effects" evaluations of Title I (now Chapter I) programs also found that participants' scores on standardized reading and mathematics tests were about 15 to 20 percent better than those of similarly needy students. The program was particularly effective for younger children in grades one to three. In fact, during the school year, they learned at rates that were almost equal to those of more advantaged youth. These gains are impressive when one considers that, on average, Title I expenditures were only $600 per student and that the special reading teachers who worked with these students were generally left to their own devices.[86] Another elementary school program, Follow-Through, also yielded significant academic gains for its participants.[87]

The results of nine-, thirteen-, and seventeen-year-olds on the reading tests of the National Assessment of Educational Progress show that while the achievement gap between white and black youth remains large, it narrowed considerably between 1971 and 1984. For example, among nine-year-olds, the gap was forty-five points in 1971 but declined to thirty-two points by 1984 (see Table 9).[88] These gains have been attributed by some analysts to desegregation efforts and to the effects of preschool and Title I programs.

Evidence from dozens of studies of programmed instruction, mastery learning, and computer-assisted instruction suggests that these approaches can also increase the skills of disadvantaged students. For

Table 9 Mean reading proficiency scores, and point change, of 9-, 13-, and 17-year-olds, by race, type of community, and parental education: 1971–1984

Variable	9-Year-Olds			13-Year-Olds			17-Year-Olds		
	1971	1984	Change 1971–84	1971	1984	Change 1971–84	1971	1984	Change 1971–84
Race									
White	214.4	220.1	+5.70	260.1	263.4	+3.30	290.4	294.6	+4.20
Black	169.3	188.4	+19.10	220.3	236.8	+16.50	240.6	263.5	+22.90
Hispanic	182.9[a]	193.0	+10.10	231.1[a]	239.2	+8.10	254.7[a]	268.7	+14.00
Achievement gap[a] (White–Black)	45.10	31.70	−13.40	39.80	26.60	−13.20	49.80	31.10	−18.70
Type of community									
Advantaged urban	231.3	231.4	+.1	272.4	274.7	+2.30	303.5	300.8	−2.70
Disadvantaged urban	177.8	194.4	+16.60	232.4	239.6	+7.20	259.4	265.9	+6.50
Rural	200.7	205.8	+5.10	245.0	255.5	+10.50	275.8	282.8	+6.40
Achievement gap[a] (Adv. Urban–Disadv. Urban)	53.50	37.00	−16.50	40.00	35.10	−4.90	44.10	34.90	−9.20
Achievement gap[a] (Adv. Urban–Rural)	30.60	25.60	−5.00	27.40	19.20	−8.20	27.70	18.00	−9.70
Parental education									
High school graduates	209.0	211.4	+2.40	255.4	253.8	−1.60	282.9	280.6	−2.30
Non-graduates	188.6	197.1	+8.50	236.2	241.5	+5.30	263.4	269.5	+6.10
Post high school	224.7	224.3	−.40	269.7	268.4	−1.30	300.9	300.0	−.90
Achievement gap[a] High school graduates and non-graduates	20.40	14.30	−6.10	19.20	12.30	−6.90	19.50	11.10	−8.40

[a] Data for 1974—not available for 1971.

Source: National Assessment of Educational Progress, *The Reading Report Card: Progress Toward Excellence in our Schools: Trends in Reading over Four National Assessments, 1971–1984*, National Assessment of Educational Progress, Report No. 15R-01 (Princeton, 1985). Constructed from tables appearing on pp. 65–71.

example, the Congressional Office of Technology Assessment concluded that computer-assisted instruction can dramatically and cost-effectively raise the scores of most students, if for no other reason than that it is an effective means of doubling the number of exercises that a student can complete in the average school year.[89] For similar reasons, and as an antidote to ability grouping and tracking in elementary and secondary schools, John Goodlad has called for an emphasis on mastery learning—whereby lessons are broken into very small units of instruction and students are not allowed to move onto the next lesson until they have demonstrated subject mastery.[90]

The Summer Training and Education Project (STEP)

Early results from this program serving fourteen- to fifteen-year-old economically disadvantaged youths also show that disadvantaged children can learn. STEP is a five-site pilot demonstration project designed to overcome the problem of summer learning loss. Operated jointly by school officials and employment and training staff, using funds from the federally funded summer jobs program, STEP provides fourteen- and fifteen-year-olds who are behind in school with a half-day of work experience (more than eighty hours over the summer) and a half-day of intensive remedial education (ninety hours), as well as eighteen hours of "life-planning instruction."[91]

Cooperating schools generally provide academic credit for gains made during the summer, and during the school year they provide follow-up activities to help young people sustain these gains. To maintain student interest, instruction had to be different from what was offered during the regular school year. The remediation is individualized and computer-assisted where possible, and the life-planning instruction makes connections between the cost of raising a family, the job needed to support it, the education necessary to obtain such a job, and the effect of an early pregnancy on life goals.

Although STEP is not easy to implement effectively, the results from its first two summers are very encouraging. At the end of the 1986 cohort's first summer, youth in the control group (who participated in work experience only) lost between three-quarters and a full grade equivalent of the gains they made in reading during the school year, and they lost about one-half of a grade equivalent in mathematics.[92] STEP participants, on the other hand, lost less in reading (only .3 of a grade equivalent) and actually gained a little (.2 of a grade equivalent) in mathematics. The net difference in performance between the experimental and control groups was .6 of a grade equivalent in reading and .8 of a grade equivalent in math. Black and Hispanic youth have done especially well. It is also encouraging that STEP participants demonstrated increased knowledge about contraceptive practices and reported less sexual activity than controls. Among those who were sexually active (more than half the sample at the project's start), STEP participants were 53 percent more likely than controls to report that they practiced contraception.

Although it is still too early to know whether these gains will be sustained, it is worth considering their implications. If improvements in academic achievement do in fact hold the key to young people's perceptions of their future life options, then the differences STEP has begun to make may be sufficient to affect the long-term school dropout, teenage parenting, and youth unemployment rates of participants. Moreover, findings of the STEP project suggest that if we could intervene in two or three of the eleven summers spaced throughout a student's elementary and secondary career, we should be able to obtain at least a grade level of improvement, simply by reducing the amount of time teachers have to spend each year reteaching what students forgot during the summers. Furthermore, funding for such a program could be drawn from the existing federal summer jobs program, a $700 million per year program that employs 650,000 disadvantaged youth each summer, nearly all of whom are behind in school, and about one-third of whom can be expected to become teenage parents.

The Military's Project 100,000

During the Vietnam War, the military recruited 311,000 "low standards" men, ages eighteen to twenty, for its "Project 100,000." These were men whose test scores did not meet military entrance requirements. About half of them were given short-term remedial education, GED High School Equivalency instruction, or other off-duty opportunities for learning. In several special programs, students gained an average of 1 to 1.5 grades in tested reading ability, depending on the program and the number of instructional hours.[93] As of 1984, more than ten years later, 8,000 of these recruits were still in the military. Although none had scored above the 20th percentile on the AFQT when they were recruited, by 1984 almost all had improved their test scores. Most had completed more years of school and had obtained a high school diploma or its equivalent. Nearly one-third eventually obtained scores above the 30th percentile on the AFQT. Furthermore, Project 100,000 recruits who did not re-enlist were found to have slightly better civilian jobs, earning higher hourly wage rates than a comparison group who never enlisted in the armed services. Although it would be incorrect to attribute all of these gains to the educational activities begun in Project 100,000, since not all of the recruits participated, it seems plausible that the coupling of basic skills instruction with military training and duties was responsible for a portion of the recruits' educational improvement.[94]

The Job Corps

This federally funded, residential education and training program has produced educational gains of 1.0 to 1.5 grade equivalents in 100 hours of instruction for its participants, made up predominantly of economically disadvantaged dropouts. These educational gains are partly responsible for the success of the one-third of all Job Corps enrollees who complete a twelve- to eighteen-month program of training. Careful evaluation studies have found that, on average, Job Corps members earn $655 more annually than a comparison group of nonparticipants.[95] The Manpower Demonstration Research Corporation is currently evaluating a fifteen-site test of a similarly structured but nonresidential program called JOBSTART, which combines remedial education and occupational skills training for disadvantaged young people seventeen to twenty-one years of age with below eighth-grade reading skills. Preliminary data indicate that participants are obtaining GED diplomas at a significantly higher rate than nonparticipants.

The Comprehensive Competencies Program (CCP)

This remedial education system is now being used in 250 learning centers by a range of community-based organizations, private industry councils, secondary schools, and postsecondary institutions and organizations. It serves 30,000 youths and adults annually.[96] Its results indicate that disadvantaged students with multiple problems can learn. Most institutions use CCP in combination with other education, training, and work experience.

CCP is a system for organizing and delivering remedial education services based on approaches that have been proven effective for disadvantaged individuals. To ensure both quality of services and impact, it combines techniques learned from research in education and the social sciences with the techniques of franchising (replicating and managing multiple sites) that are used in the business world. For example, CCP uses computers to automate management, reporting, and test grading, and it maximizes the amount of time students spend on tasks by utilizing individualized, self-paced instructional materials that are goal oriented. It is also unique in its integration of all the modes of teaching, including workbooks, computer-based instruction, and audio-visual materials. For each lesson objective, there is a section in a workbook selected from the best current materials, a computer lesson, an audio-visual component, and supplementary reading materials. CCP enrollees have shown that those who have failed in other settings can achieve learning gains. They include many single parents, welfare recipients, dropouts, delinquents, and members of minority groups, and they gain an average of 1.0 grade in reading and 1.4 grades in mathematics in twenty-eight hours of total instruction time.[97] It effectively balances caring with efficiency by using a podagogic structure that maximizes the amount of time that teachers can spend with individual students.

Jobs for America's Graduates (JAG)

This formal school-to-work transition program is currently operating in thirteen states, where it is serving more than 9,000 youths annually in more than thirty communities and 275 high schools. The program primarily targets general education high school seniors who do not anticipate enrolling full-time in postsecondary education or training, whose academic performance has been average or below average, and whose in-school employment experience is limited. To build a link between education and jobs, each local JAG program provides career counseling, knowledge about the world of work, direct job-placement assistance, and nine months of follow-up services after graduation. JAG also requires that students attain a minimum level of employment competencies, and job specialists often coordinate special academic help for students with low basic skills. Some schools award academic credit for the ''world-of-work'' classes, and most classes are offered as an integral part of the school day and school year. JAG students are encouraged to join a motivational student ''Career Association,'' which builds leadership skills and provides further learning in a series of competitive activities that test student knowledge in real-world employment situations. These competitions are judged by local employers and professionals in the employment and training field.

JAG does make a difference. During the first nine months after high school graduation, its participants were more likely to be employed than comparable nonparticipants, and on average, participants have earned $800 to $1,200 more in the first year following graduation than they would have if they had not participated in JAG.[98]

Given the necessary resources, most of the model programs discussed here—high quality preschool education, the exemplary components of the Military's Project 100,000, the Job Corps, the Comprehensive Competencies Program, and Jobs for America's Graduates—can be widely replicated and implemented. Evaluations indicate that they are effective programs and can form the basis for good systems in their own right. They can also strengthen the larger education and job-training systems of which they are a part. Effective replication of particularly exemplary models, for example, the Perry Preschool program within all Head Start centers, could be an important first step in the systematic improvement of the quality and impact of all education and training programs. Unlike most model programs, many of these have demonstrated a capacity to maintain high quality beyond the demonstration phase. Teachers and students report that they feel empowered, respected, and cared for.

Systems, Standards, and Management

Although more experimentation is warranted, there is less of a problem of what to do than of how to do it on a large enough scale and on a sequential basis, so that one intervention serves as a stepping stone to the next intervention. This means moving beyond building good programs to establishing entire systems that are designed to raise the average by helping those at the bottom and eliminating the worst service deliverers. Unfortunately, we have failed to build effective systems in the past, tending, instead, to view the educational problems of the disadvantaged as problems that could simply be solved by passing new legislation and authorizing new appropriations. Implementation, however, is 90 percent of the game.

The key to building effective systems is in establishing common goals and standards. In *High School: A Report on Secondary Education in America,* Ernest Boyer, writing for the Carnegie Council for the

Advancement of Teaching, argues that "until there is consensus on student performance among educators and parents, individual schools will find it extremely difficult to improve the quality of instruction."[99] John Goodlad in *A Place Called School* expresses similar concerns about the degree of variability from school to school in curricular content and performance.[100] David Cohen notes in *The Shopping Mall High School* that practice and expectations about what should be taught, about grading, and about homework vary dramatically from school district to school district and even from student to student.[101] Most reviewers propose increased accountability or at least a common framework within which school boards, schools, and teachers can exercise appropriate autonomy and innovation while achieving predetermined common goals.

In short, there is a crisis in focus, purpose, and direction that is exacerbated by the tendency to confuse standards with an inflexible national curriculum and by the unfounded fear that standards are the first step in federal intervention in local schooling. The most recent wave of education reforms implicitly acknowledges that standards are a prerequisite for improving children's academic performance. Governors are now proposing educational standards and are planning to take over bankrupt schools. Chief state school officers have voted to support standardized testing that will allow comparative school assessment. Colleges have begun uniform assessments of graduates' mastery of the material taught, and state Job Training Coordinating Councils are setting competency standards for the nation's job-training system. When taken together, these measures could begin to build effective systems.

Standardized tests should be administered regionally, if not nationally, because labor markets do not respect the boundaries of local school boards. Disadvantaged youth frequently are forced to confront this fact when it is too late. Without comparable standards, diplomas for inner-city high school graduates often have only marginal meaning. With better information about the actual capacity of potential new hires, employers could more effectively reward the best students with better jobs and higher pay. Such practices would probably stimulate students to take more interest in their school performance. Because employers do not currently have access to school records, students cannot see much of a relationship between school performance and working.[102]

Establishing standards for performance would be futile unless the appropriate officials have the courage to close those schools or employment and training programs that fall in the bottom 10 percent of the distribution for three years in a row. In our worst urban schools, for example, the culture of absenteeism, drug abuse, violence, and disruption may be so pernicious that the only option is to close the school, disperse the students, remove the principal, and then reopen it a year or two later with extra professional staff and only the tenth grade. Each year, a new grade could be added. In that way, a new school culture could be built, one that valued and supported learning, discipline, homework, and high expectations for student performance. New York City has such a policy but it has not implemented it consistently or with adequate forethought and planning.

Advanced Placement (AP)

The focus that comes from knowing what students need to learn and then testing them on those subjects can have a powerful effect. A handful of inner-city high schools have developed Advanced Placement (AP) programs that challenge students previously thought to be incapable of handling intellectually demanding courses. Originally the province of elite private and public schools, the AP program is a set of three-hour tests for high school students who have completed special courses to earn college credits in various fields. With those credits, they can skip introductory courses and move directly into more advanced courses in college. The results appear remarkable, both for the students enrolled in the AP program and for the overall student body.

The James A. Garfield High School in East Los Angeles, with a predominantly disadvantaged, minority student body, was able to prepare 93 students for the AP tests in calculus last May. With 84 percent of these students obtaining a passing grade, Garfield High School was responsible for more than 17 percent of all Mexican Americans nationwide who took the AP test, 24 percent of all Mexican Americans who passed the AP exam, and 32 percent of those who passed the BC exam, a more difficult version of the test. Garfield prepared more students for the AP calculus exam than all but six other public high schools in the nation, all of which select their students on a competitive basis. The AP program affects only about 15 percent of Garfield's students directly, but in the last few years, reading and mathematics scores have gradually begun to improve for all the students in the school.[103]

Standards for Teachers

The 1986 Carnegie Report, *A Nation Prepared: Teachers for the 21st Century,* recommended standards for teachers that would be developed by a National Board for Professional Teaching Standards. Using a variety of measures, including peer observations, these assessment standards would:

> . . . enable the Board to judge the quality of candidates' general education, their mastery of the subjects they teach, their knowledge of good teaching practices in general and their mastery of techniques required to teach specific subjects.[104]

As Albert Shanker, president of the American Federation of Teachers and a member of the Carnegie Commission, noted, "the current situation is a mess; each of the fifty states has its own licensing standards, and individual school districts often ignore even these low standards."[105] By establishing a uniformly high standard, the national certification system proposed by the Carnegie Commission would enable the public to identify teachers who meet specified standards, offer school boards a recognizable standard for improving and rewarding competent teachers, and provide a common measure for assessing the quality of teacher-training programs. Shanker believes that schools with few board-certified teachers are likely to see enrollments decline as people look elsewhere, and that teachers' colleges whose graduates fail to meet board standards will be forced to improve or to go out of business.

Society should reward teachers and principals who succeed. Lester Thurow has proposed that the federal government or the states establish a bonus pool of $10 billion to reward those teachers whose students surpass national norms for like students.[106] Local school boards could choose to ignore the national standards, but by doing so they would also have no claim to the bonuses. The prospect of better pay and recognition seems likely to attract many of our best students back into the teaching profession.

Employment and Training Programs

Schools generally operate within a common framework. At the state and district level, there is some general agreement about what subjects will be covered, in what order, and what materials will be used. By comparison, local employment and training programs are less likely to have common systems in place. Yet as Robert Taggart, an employment and training expert, convincingly demonstrates, the employment and training programs that have been most effective—CCP, Supported Work, Ventures in Community Improvement, and Jobs for America's Graduates—all have one thing in common. Those that operate in multiple sites have a central body that establishes standards, maintains quality control, trains and certifies local staff, and selects common materials and tests.[107]

Dozens, even hundreds, of sites operating the same model can help each other. When one program either is not performing well or has been having problems in a particular area, staff can contact or visit other sites where an experienced person can provide relevant help. The technical assistance of peers is much more valuable than generalized help from a Washington-based provider of technical assistance and training. The fact is that most teachers, trainers, and counselors operate in isolation and have little opportunity for professional enrichment and no time to stay abreast of the latest equipment, techniques, or materials. When second-chance education and training programs belong to a national or state-based network, the central body can perform that function for them and provide additional professional opportunities. The Comprehensive Competencies Program (CCP) has done this for remedial education, Ventures in Community Improvement (VICI) has done it for construction-trades training, Jobs for America's Graduates (JAG) has done it for school-to-work transition, and the Bay State Skills Corporation has begun to do it in various vocational fields.

For twenty years now, policy makers have debated whether local or federal officials know best, whether centralization or decentralization of planning and administration works best. As a result, the pendulum has continually swung from one extreme to the other. But this is a false choice. Neither local people nor federal people know best. One approach leads to re-inventing the wheel and the other frequently stifles creativity. The franchise programming models described above represent the optimal mix of centralized accountability, networking, and quality control. Franchises also encourage local flexibility, leadership, and creativity. The average results obtained by these franchised programs always exceed the average obtained by many independent, unconnected local programs. Because these problems involve large numbers, we must use multiple-site management approaches to raise programs' average quality. It is as important to keep the poor performers from falling through the floor as it is to ensure that the stars can rise to the top.

Accountability

By setting common standards and measures for assessing student and teacher performance in schools, teacher-training institutions, and job-training programs, we can take the first step toward holding these establishments accountable. The fear, of course, is that standards will be misused, that teachers will teach to the test, and that learning will become even more routinized than it is now. These are certainly legitimate concerns, and early experience from the educational excellence movement and the Job Training Partnership Act confirm the existence of some of these dangers (see below).

A more flexible system of accountability would demand that equal emphasis be placed on achievement and student retention. The key is to hold teachers responsible for the final product without prescribing an inflexible process that they must follow to that end. Both standardized tests and school or program retention rates can be blunt instruments. When used intelligently, however, they can also be valuable management tools for assessing progress either from year to year or against the norm for students from similar income and educational backgrounds.

The Current State of Affairs

As the baby boom of the 1970s gives way to the baby bust labor shortages of the late 1980s and early 1990s, employers, the military, and colleges have begun moving further down the queue of available young people. The group that remains to be served by the educational and employment training systems is more economically and educationally disadvantaged than either system traditionally has had to work with. At this time, the employment and training system should be increasing remediation services, broadening their outreach networks, and focusing on retaining young people in longer-term programs. Unfortunately, the Job Training Partnership Act (JTPA), which replaced the Comprehensive Employment and Training Act (CETA), has reduced funding for administration and support services. In addition, its cost-per-placement performance standards encourage sites to serve the less disadvantaged and to emphasize immediate job placement. The result is a mismatch between available program slots and youth's needs. Even though the law requires that 40 percent of all JTPA funds be spent on youth, the system has until recently consistently underspent these funds. Programs often serve the least disadvantaged in the eligible population, generally providing short-term training, placement, and counseling services, rather than making long-term investments in the most disadvantaged.[108]

Spawned by the baleful diagnoses of more than two dozen reports on schools, the excellence movement produced a similar set of results. State boards of education and local school boards moved to raise standards and to strengthen core curriculums in a simplistic and absolute way. Unlike Garfield High School, where higher standards were combined with special help and more direction, few school systems established standards that took into account the relative starting points of existing students and schools. Most relied solely on standardized academic achievement tests, ignoring other relevant yardsticks like dropout rates, attendance, and college acceptance. For example, a thirty-two-state survey of state responses to the push for excellence found only four projects focused on economically disadvantaged youth and six on underachieving youth.[109] The rest had initiated programs to help advanced students meet the new standards. The results were predictable. Dropout rates tended to increase as disadvantaged students found themselves falling even further behind.

Seeking Balance

There is inherent conflict in the dual notions of excellence and equality. Ability grouping was devised to let the fast learners surge ahead while the slow learners could work more deliberately. In practice, the inevitable result has been lower expectations for the slow learners, which in turn becomes a self-fulfilling prophecy. Concern for those who are behind necessitates a focus on the developmental as opposed to just the academic needs of youth. But developmental needs call for more counseling, more peer support, and more discussion about issues that are relevant to young people: peer pressure, sexual behavior, drugs, and lack of contact with the adult world. Yet more time devoted to these issues means less time for academic instruction.

The challenge is to balance these two sets of competing needs, not to choose one or the other. In fact, they are interrelated. Self-esteem and commitment to school are at least partly a product of achievement. Young people with higher basic skills have higher self-esteem than those with low skills. Logic suggests that if we can help young people catch up to their peers academically, they will evidence a stronger commitment to school. Young people themselves acknowledge the central importance of education for their younger siblings, suggesting that they see its value for themselves as well, and young single parents cite high school graduation and a good education as critical goals for their children.[110] When dropouts enroll in second-chance programs to obtain an equivalency degree or learn an occupational skill, they often report that the staff in their previous schools did not care as much about them or help them as often as the teachers and counselors in second-chance programs.[111]

The economic, demographic, and cultural changes that have occurred over the past few decades have increased the importance of caring and committed staffs. Since the start of the postwar period, the primary adult labor market has had less and less use for young people under the age of twenty and for less educated adults.[112] At the same time, work in the youth-oriented labor market is fragmented, often low-skilled, and often age-segregated. Thus it has become more difficult for young people to see what adults do in the workplace. Adult role models for disadvantaged young people have been further limited by the growing prevalence of single-parent families among the poor and the movement of a growing number of middle-class minority families from the inner cities to the suburbs. Taken together, these developments and others such as the growth of two-worker families have added to the demands placed on schools as surrogate parents, demands they have been hard pressed to meet during the back-to-basics movement.

It does not follow, however, that our schools have deteriorated in some absolute sense in recent years. Dropout rates have not increased appreciably; rather, they have simply stopped declining and remain well above average for minority and economically disadvantaged youth.[113] Similarly, the decline in test scores among nine-, thirteen- and seventeen-year-olds that occurred in the 1960s and early 1970s has now reversed itself, although test scores appear to be leveling off for younger youth. What has changed, however, is the demands that technology and the economy have placed on the schools. These demands have increased at a rate that schools alone have been unable to meet.

To fill the needs of today's young people, a range of community institutions, from the Urban League to Scouts, from Boys and Girls Clubs to employment and training programs, must be recognized and supported. These provide valuable opportunities for out-of-school and out-of-family learning. Also valuable are organized team sports, cooperative education programs that blend youth into adult work settings, expanded apprenticeship opportunities, summer jobs in structured work settings, and community service and conservation corps programs. They provide opportunities for teens to interact with adults and to observe the world of work.[114] Historically, the employment and training system has been a major funder of these opportunities for community learning and personal development. This interest should continue.

An Agenda

The new demographics of the youth population add a new urgency and a new dimension to the education and training tasks that lie before us. Because these are large problems, it is essential that we begin now to push for immediate changes in both the educational and the job-training systems of our nation. Long-term objectives should include establishing appropriate standards with bonuses and other incentives to reward high-performing schools, teachers, and students; lengthening the school year; and creating and implementing effective training programs. To close the domestic and foreign achievement gaps among young people, we will have to do the following:

- Focus our efforts on all children, but give special attention to economically disadvantaged and minority children who are deficient in both basic skills and higher-order thinking skills.
- Offer a continuum of services for both parents and children in recognition of the intergenerational causes of low basic skills.
- Address the phenomenon of summer learning loss, especially during the neglected middle school years when students learn the basic academic skills they will need for a lifetime of learning and working.
- Develop standards that hold local institutions accountable while leaving room for local officials to exercise autonomy.
- Smooth the transition from school to work for high school graduates who are not college bound.
- Improve the quality and availability of the nation's second-chance job-training and community college programs.

To meet these needs we will have to strengthen ties between the schools and the second-chance job-training and community college programs. What are some of the things that local school officials and employment/training staff can do?

Appoint a prominent committee to assess both state and city policies and programs dealing with human resources and education. In the past few years, most localities have witnessed a proliferation of initiatives—literacy training, new community college programs, special training and education projects, dropout- and teenage pregnancy-prevention programs, new vocational education programs, etc. Concurrently, we have seen the expansion of local preschool systems without adequate standards or a clear articulation of their connection to elementary school. In the upper grades, we have failed to connect the school, job-training, and community college systems through such basic steps as formalizing the options open to sixteen- to eighteen-year-olds who have achieved some agreed-upon minimum level of competence, and wish to move on to other education and training opportunities.

The committee should begin by making a simple statement of mission, philosophy, and objectives for the human resource system. It should assess the quality of education, training, and employment-related activities; study the effects and cost-effectiveness of alternative intervention strategies; assess existing management information systems, purchasing procedures, tests, and materials; develop a comprehensive picture of the present health of the community's economy and its future human resource needs; determine the work force's current and potential deficiencies; and finally, compare the human resource system's capabilities with the area's future needs. Next, the committee could initiate a plan to streamline the system, eliminate duplication, and encourage integration, joint staff training, and common assessment and evaluation systems.

Boston, Portland, Minneapolis, and a handful of states have begun strategic planning initiatives of this kind.[115] Their success will depend upon the ability of the planning group to turn the initiative into a management task rather than a political exercise. The central explanation for the success of the Boston Compact has been its ability to unite the business community behind the school superintendent and the head of the Private Industry Council. This has enabled all to carry out their responsibilities with minimal political interference.

Match federal job-training dollars at the state and local levels. A first step would be to permit the per student average daily attendance dollars that states allocate to local school districts to follow individual students who drop out and then enter alternative schools and job-training programs. Oregon and other states already have laws on the books that authorize such a funding stream. Schools and employment and training programs might then be expected to compete for the attention of dropout youth. Such a system would increase public choice and ensure that students could take an active role in securing for themselves a high-quality elementary and secondary education. Eventually, new financing arrangements will be needed that unite Basic Educational Opportunity Grants for postsecondary training with college scholarships and loan funds. In such a system, all young people might have access to a fixed-dollar individual training account that would be replenished from a tax on their future earnings. These funds could be used by both graduates and dropouts for second-chance program enrollment as well as for postsecondary training and education.

Make education an integral part of the employment and training services mix. At the moment, JTPA Title IIA funds remain underspent, and the available evidence indicates that the system is continuing to emphasize short-term counseling and placement services instead of long-term investments in education and training. As a result, JTPA is still not reaching those most in need. To redress this imbalance, we must go where the youth are—to the streets and the schools. Community organizations must play a role in any strategy of recruiting those most in need. Intensive remedial education efforts are needed, either by establishing schools-within-schools or education-training centers to substitute for schools for dropout youth and adults. The Colorado and Texas Basic Skills Investment Corporations have begun just such initiatives.[116] We need to build a network of supplementary, academy-type opportunities similar to the Juku schools of the Japanese, for both advantaged and disadvantaged youth.

Double the size of Job Corps and Head Start over five years. This would be one way to address the literacy needs of both disadvantaged parents and their children, emphasizing quality and requiring that both programs build in ties to the local service community. For example, all Head Start directors might be trained in the Perry Preschool approach to early childhood care and education and then be encouraged to train home-care providers in the same approach so that we can reach the 70 percent of all poor children who are not now enrolled in preschool programs. Head Start's parent-education programs should also be upgraded. In this way, Head Start centers could serve as the focal point for all child care and early education in a community. A similar relationship should be built between the Job Corps and young adult education and training programs. The potential of such programs is now being tested in Manpower Demonstration Research Corporation's JOBSTART program.

Construct a system of summer education opportunities. These could begin with follow-through programs in mathematics and reading during the elementary school years; continue with advanced science, mathematics, and literature courses for high-potential but low-achieving junior high school youth; combine summer jobs and remediation programs, funded with Chapter I and JTPA Title IIB summer job dollars, for disadvantaged fourteen- and fifteen-year-olds who have substantial skill deficits; and conclude with advanced Upward Bound programs for college-bound, disadvantaged high school students.

The first task would be to redesign the summer jobs program by targeting fourteen- to sixteen-year-olds (who do not have the job opportunities that seventeen- and eighteen-year-olds have) and mandating that all participants receive intensive remedial education. The second task would be to construct a comprehensive system of quality summer learning out of the network of thousands of pre-college programs in science, mathematics, and engineering that evolved in the 1960s.[117] Reversing summer learning loss and converting the summer into a season of learning gains is an important opportunity for educational reformers.

All of these summer programs should include life-planning curricula and counseling. Schools should reward gains made during the summer. Strong summer programs could be a step toward year-round schooling and toward closer ties between schools and training institutions.

Establish school-to-work transition services as an integral part of the high school curriculum for the 30 to 40 percent of young people who are not going on to postsecondary education and/or training. These programs should require minimum levels of educational competency and provide knowledge of job requirements, appropriate job behavior, and the labor market. Evidence from the Jobs for America's Graduates' school-to-work transition program indicates that participants are more likely than nonparticipants to be employed after high school graduation.

Build a strong vocational training, retraining, and apprenticeship system. Such a system should offer training opportunities in a broader array of occupations, give employers a central role in the design of its programs, and serve all Americans equally. An expanded apprenticeship system could smooth the school-to-work transition for high school seniors who do not enroll in college, bolster their vocational and academic skills, and provide employers with a more highly skilled and productive work force in the long run. During the past two decades, a smaller proportion of young high school graduates has been able to secure full-time jobs in the first year following graduation. This has been particularly true among young black high school graduates. Only one of every four young black high school graduates under the age of twenty and not enrolled in college was able to acquire a full-time job in March 1986.

Efforts to strengthen the nation's training system will require a variety of actions. At present, employers are reluctant to invest heavily in entry-worker training because they fear that workers will leave after the company trains them. Furthermore, the vocational high school, community college, and private proprietary training systems are often outdated and, as the Federal Trade Commission has stated, many of the proprietary schools have only limited success in placing graduates. A new system must be forged out of the existing hodgepodge of schools and training programs. The German "dual system" of apprenticeships that combine on-the-job and classroom training could serve as the model for our efforts in this field.

Consider passing a national technology-investment act designed to help nonprofit organizations purchase new equipment, materials, and technologies that have proven effective in improving education and training. The Ford Foundation has invested $1.5 million in a revolving loan fund that enabled the Remediation and Training Institute (RTI) to purchase in bulk the computers, books, and courseware required in CCP learning centers. RTI was able to save 40 to 60 percent and then to pass on this saving, less interest and administrative costs, to local CCP learning centers. Centers pay for the equipment on a lease-purchase basis over three years, using funds from contracts awarded by local JTPA and other agencies that support the education of disadvantaged students.

Devote space in public housing projects to programs aimed at enhancing the life options of their residents. Each project would have a parent-child center for children under three years of age, a high-quality preschool program, an IBM "Writing to Read" program for elementary school youth, a summer follow-through program, a complete CCP learning center with curricula from beginning readers to pre-college, and a program like Supported Work or Ventures in Community Improvement to train housing project residents in the maintenance and repair of their buildings. Public housing projects are among the most dismal places in America. Implemented on an experimental basis in five locations, a combination of programs like this would provide an opportunity to learn more about multiple interventions over the life cycle. If these effects are additive, they will help to break the cycle of transferring deficient skills—and, hence, poverty, dependency, and underemployment—from generation to generation.

Finally, we must begin now to change young people's future expectations. By 1995 there will be approximately one-fourth fewer eighteen- to twenty-four-year-olds than there were in 1979. The implications for employers, colleges, and the military are extraordinary and can already be seen in the multitude of help-wanted signs in many U.S. fast-food establishments, particularly in areas with low unemployment. Today the armed services take about one in five of the available pool of eligible males. By 1995 they will need nearly one of every three.

The presidents of a major company and a college, along with a high-ranking military officer, should visit the sixth grade graduating class of every elementary school in America to help young people realize that they will be in demand. We have all heard of the excitement generated by the "I Have a Dream Project," but few of us realize that the National Guard provides practically a full college scholarship plus a monthly salary to any qualified enlistee who also wants to go to college. This is a substantially larger commitment than the "I Have a Dream" millionaires have been able to make.

Conclusion

This has been a long story. The national economy has undergone a difficult period of stagnation in real wages and family income precipitated by the convergence of several factors: the oil price shocks, low productivity growth, the baby-boom generation's entry into the work force, declines in the growth of real investment expenditures, rampant inflation, and back-to-back recessions. There has also been an accelerated transition to a service economy with its very different occupational mix, skills requirements, and wage structure. During this same period, the United States lost the dominant position it held after World War II. We no longer have the best educated or the most literate work force, nor do we have a clear lead in science and technology.

These changes have had a devastating effect on the real earnings of young male adult workers, especially those with limited education and skills. As their real earnings have declined, their marriage rates have plummeted. Out-of-wedlock childbearing has increased as a consequence, exacerbating the prevalence of poverty among children. Fortunately, however, the oil price shocks, the baby boom, and the severe inflation of the late 1970s and early 1980s are behind us. Yet if we are to get real wages and family incomes growing again in this new world order, we will have to increase our productivity, which in turn requires that we get control of our national and private debts and begin to invest in people, plants, and research. Education and training are an important part of that process.

Our task will be complicated by new demographics. There will be fewer young workers and a higher proportion of our work force will come from disadvantaged backgrounds. This situation represents a window of opportunity while also posing a challenge of immense proportions. To have a high-quality work force that is competitive internationally, we will have to improve the academic and vocational skills of those at the bottom of the ladder.

The case for basic skills does not end with national economic needs. There is extensive evidence that skills deficiencies are significant factors in such persistent and costly antisocial behavior as teenage parenting and dropping out of school, both of which contribute to dependency and poverty in future generations. Although basic skills deficiencies are not the only cause of these problems and remediation strategies should not be our only response, no human resource program aimed at these problems can ignore the need for basic skills training.

It is important to stress the fact that none of the initiatives described here can make a difference in the basic skills crisis if they are not of high quality and tied to a continuum of other educational, training, and support services. We must also be careful to develop and use new standards that will stimulate the performance of all young people. To ensure that those who most need better schooling and second-chance employment and training services get their fair share of effective help, we must close schools and programs that perform poorly and begin new ones. Finally, standards are no substitute for caring, high expectations, and hard work.

Although the case for improving basic skills is overwhelming, there is a much simpler and probably more reliable test for confirming how important they are as an underlying cause and a necessary part of any solution to many of our most pressing national problems. That litmus test is simple: If your child were falling behind in school, would you think it important to get him or her extra academic help in the evening, the weekends, and during the summer? If we as a nation want to begin improving our rate of real economic growth, restoring growth in real wages and real family incomes, and reducing poverty and disparities in the incomes of various racial and ethnic groups, we should do no less for all of our nation's children.

Notes

Earlier versions of this paper were delivered by Andrew Sum in October 1986 at the Annual Conference of the Comprehensive Competencies Program in Grand Junction, Colorado, and by Gordon Berlin in December 1986 at a Conference of School and Employment and Training Officials sponsored by the National Governors' Association and the Chief State School Officers in Washington, D.C.

1. The National Commission on Excellence in Education, *A Nation at Risk: The Imperative for Educational Reform* (Washington, D.C.: U.S. Government Printing Office, 1983).

2. National Research Council, *Risking the Future: Adolescent Sexuality, Pregnancy and Childbearing* (Washington, D.C.: National Academy Press, 1986).

3. Committee for Economic Development, *Strategy for U.S. Industrial Competitiveness* (New York: Committee for Economic Development, 1984).

4. During the first five months of 1987, major stories on American economic competitiveness were carried in the following national and international magazines: "Washington's Big Worry: Can the U.S. Compete?" *Newsweek,* January 19, 1987; "Making America Compete," *The Economist,* February 21–27, 1987; "Can America Compete?" *Business Week,* April 20, 1987; "Can America Compete?" *The Washington Post,* National Weekly Edition, May 4, 1987.

5. For example, see: Levy, Frank and Richard C. Michel, "An American Bust for the Baby Boom," *Challenge,* March-April 1986, pp. 33–39; Danziger, Sheldon and Peter Gottschalk, "Families with Children Have Fared Worst," *Challenge,* March-April 1986, pp. 40–47; and Thurow, Lester C., *The Zero-Sum Solution: Building a World-Class American Economy* (New York: Simon and Schuster, Inc., 1986).

6. U.S. Bureau of the Census, Current Population Reports, Series P-60, No. 151, *Money Income of Households, Families, and Persons in the U.S.: 1984* (Washington, D.C.: U.S. Government Printing Office, 1986). To maintain consistency with some of the other data sources used in this paper most of the comparisons used in this paper are from 1984. The Census Bureau's most recent figures for 1986 show that inflation-adjusted median family income, having risen 10.7 percent since 1982, has barely recovered to levels last reached in 1973 and 1978.

7. For a more detailed look at recent trends in the real earnings of young men, their marriage behavior, out-of-wedlock births, and poverty among young families, see: Johnson, Clifford and Andrew Sum, *Declining Earnings of Young Men: Their Relation to Poverty, Teen Pregnancy and Family Formation* (Washington, D.C.: Children's Defense Fund, May 1987).

8. For further discussion of these issues, see: Denison, Edward, *Trends in American Economic Growth, 1929–1982* (Washington, D.C.: Brookings Institution, 1985); Levy, Frank, *Dollars and Dreams: The Changing American Income Distribution* (New York: Russell Sage Foundation, Basic Books, 1987); Thurow, Lester, *The Zero-Sum Solution* (New York: Simon and Schuster, 1985); Levitan, Sar and Diane Werneke, *Productivity, Problems and Prospects* (Baltimore: Johns Hopkins University Press, 1984); Economic Policy Institute, *Proceedings of a Seminar on Declining American Incomes and Living Standards* (Washington, D.C., May 1986).

9. Output per hour of work can be measured for the entire private business sector or for the nonfarm business sector. Since agricultural productivity was rising faster than that of the nonfarm sector during the 1947–73 period, the annual rate of productivity growth in the private business sector was nearly one-half of a percentage point higher than that of the nonfarm business sector. The annual average rates of growth in productivity for these two sectors during the 1947–73 period were 2.9 percent and 2.4 percent, respectively.

   See U.S. Council of Economic Advisers, Table B-37, *1980 Economic Report of the President* (Washington, D.C.: U.S. Government Printing Office, 1980), p. 32.

10. Productivity of workers in the nonfarm business sector of the U.S. economy increased by only 9.4 percent between 1973 and 1986, representing an annual average increase of only .7 percent. During the preceding thirteen-year period, output per hour in the nonfarm business sector expanded by 35.8 percent, an annual rate of growth of nearly

2.4 percent. Although productivity in most manufacturing industries has improved markedly in the 1980s, gains have been far lower in other industrial sectors. In key retail trade industries, such as grocery stores, drug stores, and eating and drinking places, productivity of workers is estimated to have actually declined between 1980 and 1985.

See U.S. Department of Labor, Bureau of Labor Statistics, Table 44, *Monthly Labor Review,* April 1987, p. 102; Herman, Arthur S., "Productivity Gains Continued in Many Industries During 1985," *Monthly Labor Review,* April 1987, pp. 48–52.

11. Similar sharp breaks occurred in the growth trend of real Gross Domestic Product (GDP) per hour worked in the U.S. Between 1950 and 1973 real GDP per hour worked rose by 75 percent, or approximately 2.5 percent per year. Between 1973 and 1984 real GDP per hour increased by only 11 percent, or less than 1 percent per year. Our annual growth rate in real GDP per hour over this eleven-year period was only one-third to one-fourth as high as that of our major West European and Japanese competitors.

See Maddison, Angus, "Growth and Slowdown in Advanced Capitalist Economies: Techniques of Quantitative Assessment," *The Journal of Economic Literature,* Volume 25, Number 2, June 1987, pp. 649–698.

12. Levy, Frank, *Dollars and Dreams.*

13. *Ibid.*

14. *Ibid.*

15. Governor Orr's remarks appeared in Broder, David S., "Take It From the Governors," *The Washington Post,* National Weekly Edition, March 9, 1987, p. 4.

16. U.S. Bureau of the Census, Current Population Reports, Series P-60, No. 157, *Money Income and Poverty Status of Families and Persons in the United States: 1986* (Washington, D.C.: U.S. Government Printing Office, 1987).

17. Thurow, Lester C., *The Zero-Sum Solution,* p. 82.

18. When older workers are displaced from their jobs as a result of plant shutdowns or major reductions in force, they tend to experience far greater difficulties in securing any type of job and, when reemployed, incur larger relative wage declines.

See Flaim, Paul O. and Ellen Sehgal, "Displaced Workers of 1979–83: How Have They Fared?" *Monthly Labor Review,* June 1985, pp. 3–16.

19. For example, between 1973 and 1984 the percentage of all men twenty to twenty-four years old with no reported income increased by only 2 percentage points, from 5 percent to 7 percent; however, among black men, the proportion with no reported income rose from 8 percent in 1973 to 20 percent in 1984. It should be noted that the cash income of an individual includes more than earnings from self-employment or wage and salary employment. For young males, however, the vast bulk of their payments represents earnings, since they receive few transfer incomes and have little property income. For example, in 1973 the mean earnings of all twenty- to twenty-four-year-old males accounted for 96 percent of their mean incomes. By 1984 this ratio was approximately 92 percent.

    See Sum, Andrew and Neal Fogg, "Trends in the Real Incomes and Earnings of Young Males in the U.S.: 1967–1985," Working Paper, Center for Labor Market Studies, Northeastern University, 1987.

20. These and similar numbers reported in this paper on earnings, incomes, and marriage patterns were derived from the March 1974 and March 1985 Current Population Survey Public Use Tapes. Calculations were performed by the Center for Labor Market Studies at Northeastern University and are presented in tabular form in a number of technical papers written by Andrew Sum, the center's director, and Neal Fogg.

21. See Wilson, William, *The Declining Significance of Race* (Chicago: University of Chicago Press, 1980); Kilson, Martin, "Black Social Class and the Intergenerational Transfer of Poverty," *The Public Interest*, No. 64, Summer 1981, pp. 58–78.

22. See, for example: National Academy of Sciences, National Academy of Engineering, Institute of Medicine, *High School and the Changing Workplace: The Employers' View*, Report of the Panel on Secondary School Education for the Changing Workplace (Washington, D.C.: National Academy Press, 1984); Johnston, William and Arnold Packer, *Workforce 2000, American Work and Workers in the 21st Century* (Indianapolis: Hudson Institute, 1987); Education Commission of the States, *Action for Excellence: A Comprehensive Plan to Improve our Nation's Schools* (Denver, 1983); National Association of Manufacturers, *America's Human Resources* (Washington, D.C.: Perspectives on National Issues, April 1982).

23. Jencks, Christopher, et al., Chapter 4, *Who Gets Ahead: The Determinants of Economic Success in America* (New York: Basic Books, 1979), p. 119.

24. Hunter, John E., "Cognitive Ability, Cognitive Aptitudes, Job Knowledge, and Job Performance," *Journal of Vocational Behavior,* Vol. 29, No. 3, December 1986, pp. 340–362.

25. House, Ernest A. and William Madula, "Race, Gender and Jobs— Losing Ground on Employment," University of Colorado at Boulder, Laboratory for Policy Studies, Boulder, Colo., April 1987.

26. U.S. Department of Labor, Bureau of Labor Statistics, Table 20, *Monthly Labor Review,* April 1987, p. 84.

27. Bluestone, Barry and Bennett Harrison, *The Great American Job Machine,* report prepared for the U.S. Congress, Joint Economic Committee, December 1986.

28. Sum, Andrew and Neal Fogg, "Industrial Change and Its Impacts on the Employment, Real Earnings, and Marriage Behavior of Young Adult Men," Center for Labor Market Studies, Northeastern University, 1987.

29. These estimates are based on the 1973 earnings distribution of all white and black male dropouts and the March 1985 race-specific marriage rates for white and black male high school dropouts in each earnings category.

    See Sum, Andrew and Neal Fogg, "Real Earnings of Young Men and Trends in the Marriage Behavior of Young Adult Males in the U.S.," working paper, Center for Labor Market Studies, Northeastern University, 1987.

30. See Garfinkel, Irwin and Sara S. McLanahan, Chapter 3, *Single Mothers and Their Children: A New American Dilemma* (Washington, D.C.: Urban Institute Press, 1986); Congressional Research Service and Congressional Budget Office, Chapter 3, *Children in Poverty,* report prepared for the Committee on Ways and Means, U.S. House of Representatives (Washington, D.C.: U.S. Government Printing Office, 1985); Danziger, Sandra, "Breaking the Chains: From Teenage Girls to Welfare Mothers," Chapter 5 in Jack A. Meyer, ed., *Ladders Out of Poverty* (Washington, D.C.: American Horizons Foundation, 1987).

    Danziger reports that teenage births among both blacks and whites have declined significantly. Between 1960 and 1982 the number of births per thousand among white teens fell from 79.4 to 44.6. The number of black teen births fell from 196.1 per thousand to 97.0. The alarm over teenage childbearing arises from the fact that, in 1982, 87 percent of all births to black teens and 37 percent of births to white teens were to unwed mothers as compared to 44 percent for blacks and 17.5 percent for whites in 1970. Between 1970 and 1984 the rate of out-of-wedlock births per 1,000 unmarried women declined significantly among blacks fifteen to twenty-four but rose among whites. These teenage mothers were much more likely to become welfare dependent and to have low birth-weight babies, a precursor of higher infant mortality and retardation. Of equal concern is that pregnancy rates remain high while abortions continue to rise and account for a significant share of the overall decline in birth rates.

31. Garfinkel, Irwin and Sara McLanahan, *Single Mothers and Their Children.*

32. Sum, Andrew, Paul Harrington, and William Goedicke, "One Fifth of a Nation," *Youth and Society* (Beverly Hills: Sage Publications, March 1987), pp. 1–32.

33. Ellwood, David, *Divide and Conquer: Responsible Security for America's Poor Families,* Project on Social Welfare and the American Future, Ford Foundation, New York, 1987.

34. Garfinkel, Irwin and Sara McLanahan, *Single Mothers and Their Children.*

35. Levy, Frank, *Dollars and Dreams.*

36. Thurow, Lester, *The Zero-Sum Solution.*

37. See National Academy of Sciences, *High School and the Changing Workplace*; Lerner, Barbara, "American Education: How Are We Doing?," *The Public Interest,* Fall 1982, pp. 59–82.

38. See Ranbom, Sheppard, "Schooling in Japan," *Education Week,* February 20, February 27, and March 6, 1985; White, Merry, *The Japanese Educational Challenge: A Commitment to Children* (New York: Free Press, 1987), p.70.

39. See Rohlen, Thomas P., *Japan's High Schools* (Berkeley: University of California Press, 1983); Thurow, Lester, "A National Perspective on the Changing Economy," speech given at the Bay State Skills Corporation Conference on State Strategies for a Competitive Workforce, Boston, Mass., October 3, 1986.

40. White, Merry, *The Japanese Educational Challenge.*

41. Rohlen, Thomas P., *Japan's High Schools.*

42. *Ibid.*

43. Jones, Calvin, et al., *Four Years After High School: A Capsule Description of 1980 Seniors* (Washington, D.C.: U.S. Department of Education, Center for Statistics, August 1986).

44. See U.S. Department of Labor, Table B-9, *Manpower Report of the President* (Washington, D.C.: U.S. Government Printing Office, 1971),

pp. 244–45; U.S. Department of Labor, Bureau of Labor Statistics, *Educational Attainment of Workers, March 1982–83,* BLS Bulletin 2191 (Washington, D.C.: U.S. Government Printing Office, April 1984).

45. See U.S. Department of Commerce, Bureau of the Census, *School Enrollment—Social and Economic Characteristics of Students: October 1984* (Current Population Reports, Population Characteristics, Series P-20, No. 404; Washington, D.C.: U.S. Government Printing Office, November 1985); Kaufman, Philip, *Growth in Higher Education Enrollment: 1978 to 1985* (Washington, D.C.: U.S. Government Printing Office, 1987).

46. Johnston, William and Arnold Packer, *Workforce 2000,* pp. 3–32.

47. See Hamilton, Stephen F., "The West German Apprenticeship System," report prepared for the W.T. Grant Foundation Project on Youth in Society, 1987; Reubens, Beatrice G., *Apprenticeship in Foreign Countries,* R & D Monograph 77 (Washington, D.C.: U.S. Government Printing Office, 1980); Spring, William J., "Youth Unemployment and the Transition from School to Work," *New England Economic Review,* March/April 1987, pp. 3–16; Williams, Shirley, et al., *Youth Without Work: Three Countries Approach the Problem* (Paris: Organization for Economic Co-Operation and Development, 1982).

48. Jones, Calvin, et al., *Four Years After High School: A Capsule Description of 1980 Seniors.*

49. Reubens, Beatrice G., *Apprenticeship in Foreign Countries,* pp. 12–13. During 1977 the estimated total number of apprentices in the United States was only equal to .3 percent of total civilian employment. This ratio ranged from 5.4 percent to 6.2 percent in Austria, Germany, and Switzerland during the same year.

50. Fallows, James, "Gradgrind's Heirs," *Atlantic Monthly,* March 1987, p. 19.

51. See U.S. Department of Commerce, Bureau of the Census, *Projections of the Population in the United States: 1977–2050* (Washington, D.C.: U.S. Government Printing Office, 1977); U.S. Department of Commerce, Bureau of the Census, *Projections of the Population of the United States by Age, Sex and Race: 1983–2080* (Current Population Reports, Series P-25, No. 952; Washington, D.C.: U.S. Government Printing Office, 1984).

52. See Darling-Hammond, Linda, *Equality and Excellence: The Educational Status of Black Americans* (New York: College Entrance Examination Board, 1985); National Assessment of Educational Progress,

The Reading Report Card: Progress Toward Excellence in Our Schools. (Report No. 15-R-01; Princeton, N.J.: National Assessment of Educational Progress, 1985); Goodison, Marlene B., *A Summary of Data Collected from Graduate Record Examination Test Takers During 1980– 1981* (Princeton, N.J.: Educational Testing Service, May 1982), pp. 7– 77; Educational Testing Service, *Graduate Record Examination Data Summary Report #9* (Princeton, N.J.: Educational Testing Service, 1983–84), pp. 82–83; Rock, Donald, *Study of Excellence in High School Education: Longitudinal Study, 1980–1982* (Princeton, N.J.: Educational Testing Service, 1985); Biemiller, Lawrence, "Black Students Average Aptitude Scores up 7 Points in a Year," *The Chronicle of Higher Education,* January 1985, p. 17.

53. It should be noted that AFQT scores predict performance best when used in conjunction with high school graduation. School dropouts with high scores generally have not done well in the military. Their reenlistment rates are low and early discharge rates high. However, when the military inadvertently admitted a substantial number of low scorers who would not otherwise have been admitted, most performed satisfactorily. Because of size, and because it has a large number of jobs that do not require high skills, the military has the flexibility to accommodate some recruits with lower skills. Nevertheless, military officials contend that the growing sophistication of military equipment requires uniformly high standards of ability.

54. General ability factors appear to be the strongest predictor of job performance in a wide array of jobs from entry-level to professional-technical jobs. See Hunter, John E., "Cognitive Ability, Cognitive Aptitudes, Job Knowledge, and Job Performance," *Journal of Vocational Behavior,* Vol. 29, Number 3, December 1986, pp. 340–362; Gottfredson, Linda S., "Societal Consequences of the G Factor in Employment," *Journal of Vocational Behavior,* Vol. 29, Number 3, December 1986, pp. 379–410; Klitgaard, Robert, *Choosing Elites: Selecting the Best and Brightest at Top Universities and Elsewhere* (New York: Basic Books, 1985).

55. For recent evidence on employment problems of poor teens and black teens, see Freeman, Richard B., "Young Blacks and Jobs—What We Now Know," *The Public Interest,* Number 78, Winter 1985, pp. 18– 31; Hahn, Andrew and Robert Lerman, *What Works in Youth Employment Policy?* (Washington, D.C.: Committee on New American Realities, 1985); Sum, Andrew, Paul Harrington, and William Goedicke, "One-Fifth of A Nation: Employment Problems of Poor Youth in America," pp. 195–237.

56. Freeman, Richard B., "Young Blacks and Jobs—What We Now Know."

57. Sum, Andrew, Paul Harrington, and William Goedicke, *Basic Skills of America's Teens and Young Adults: Findings of the 1980 National ASVAB Testing and Their Implications for Education, Employment, and Training Programs* (New York: report prepared for the Ford Foundation by the Center for Labor Market Studies, Northeastern University, 1986).

58. For a recent review of the size, nature, causes, and consequences of the dropout problem, see Hahn, Andrew, Jacqueline Danzberger, and Bernard Lefkowitz, *Dropouts in America: Enough is Known for Action* (Washington, D.C.: Institute for Educational Leadership, March 1987).

59. *Ibid.*

60. Gueron, Judy, *Lessons from a Job Guarantee: The Youth Incentive Entitlement Pilot Projects* (New York: Manpower Demonstration Research Corporation, 1984).

61. See Pittman, Karen, "Model Programs: Preventing Adolescent Pregnancy and Building Youth Self-Sufficiency," Children's Defense Fund, Washington, D.C., July 1986; Moore, Kristen and Charles Betsey, *Choice and Circumstance: Racial Differences in Adolescent Sexuality and Fertility* (Brunswick, N.J.: Transaction Books, 1986); Quint, Janet C. and James Riccio, *The Challenge of Serving Pregnant and Parenting Teens* (New York: Manpower Demonstration Research Corporation, April 1985); Congressional Research Service and Congressional Budget Office, *Children in Poverty,* p. 352.

The latter report summarizes the evidence pro and con on the effects of contraceptive information in preventing pregnancy and encouraging sexual activity. They found little evidence to suggest that knowledge increases sexual activity and some information to indicate that it reduced pregnancies among previously sexually active teens. The Alan Guttmacher Institute found that the majority of teenagers came to family planning clinics after they had been sexually active for nine months or more, also suggesting that knowledge alone does not immediately reduce or result in additional sexual activity.

The Moore book reports on a series of hypothetical case examples that were read to young people from various ethnic and economic backgrounds, who were then asked to predict the outcome. One example involved a young woman from a poor family who had poor academic performance in school and whose boyfriend was pressuring her to have sex. The other example involved similar circumstances except that the girl had good grades in school and a chance to go to college. Respondents to the first example indicated that teenage pregnancy was a likely and not necessarily a bad outcome for the first girl, but they urged the second girl to say no, or use contraception, because she was viewed as having a future.

The MDRC study of Project Redirection (Quint and Riccio) was a quasi-experimental study of a counseling and service program intended to enhance the educational, job-related, parenting, and life-management skills of pregnant and parenting youths aged seventeen and under. The program at the same time encouraged these young people to delay further childbearing. While parenting teens were participating in the program, they stayed in school longer and had fewer additional children than a comparison group of nonparticipants. But two years later, no significant differences existed in the pregnancy rates of the experimental and comparison groups. MDRC is convinced that the treatment was not adequately focused on education and employment, and it is now testing a more comprehensive *direct* service model for women of eighteen to twenty-two. It is called "New Chance."

62. All of the mean test scores of blacks and Hispanics with household incomes below 125 percent of the poverty line consistently fell into the bottom 20 percent of the test distribution and in many cases fell into the bottom 10 percent of the distribution. See Venezky, Richard, Carl Kaestle, and Andrew Sum, *The Subtle Danger: Reflections on the Literacy Abilities of America's Young Adults* (Princeton, N. J.: Educational Testing Service, January 1987).

63. White and black males eighteen to twenty-four years old with AFQT test scores in the bottom fifth of the basic skills distribution for their racial groups were substantially more likely than their more highly skilled counterparts to have served time in a youth or adult correctional institution. Those males in the bottom fifth of both the black and white test score distributions were *three times* more likely than those in the middle fifth to have been sentenced to a correctional institution and *fifteen times* more likely to have been sentenced than those in the upper fifth of the skills distribution.

See Sum, Andrew and Neeta Parekh, "Criminal Charges, Arrests, Convictions, and Sentencing to Correctional Institutions Among Males (18–23) in the U.S.: 1980," working paper prepared for the Ford Foundation (New York: Center for Labor Market Studies, Northeastern University, 1986).

For a comprehensive review of research on IQ test scores and the criminal behavior of adults, see Herrnstein, Richard J., "Some Criminogenic Traits of Offenders," in *Crime and Public Policy,* ed. James Q. Wilson (San Francisco: Institute for Contemporary Studies, 1983), pp. 31–52; Wilson, James Q. and Richard J. Herrnstein, *Crime and Human Nature, The Definitive Study of the Causes of Crime* (New York: Simon and Schuster, 1985).

64. For a review of reasons cited by dropouts themselves for leaving school prior to graduation, see Hahn, Andrew and Jacqueline Danzberger, with Bernard Lefkowitz, *op. cit.,* 1987; Rock, Donald A., et al., Chapter 8, "The Dropouts versus School Stayers," *Study of Excellence in High School Education.* The two most frequently cited reasons for dropping out in the latter study were "poor grades" (33 percent) and "did not like school" (33 percent).

65. See Moore, Kristen and Charles Betsey, *Choice and Circumstance: Racial Differences in Adolescent Sexuality and Fertility*; Kirsch, Irwin S. and Ann Jungeblut, *Literacy: Profiles of America's Young Adults,* (Princeton, N. J.: Educational Testing Service, 1986), pp. C-26, C-30.

66. As Horace Mann, the first secretary of the Massachusetts Board of Education, wrote in the board's Twelfth Annual Report: "Education beyond all other devices of human origin is the great equalizer of the conditions of men . . . ," cited in Bernard Lefkowitz, *Tough Change.* By way of comparison, in 1979 Jencks et al. concluded in *Who Gets Ahead* that skills matter but " . . . the effects of test performance on earnings are not very large relative to the overall earnings gap between the rich and poor in general. Our findings, therefore, do not characterize the United States as a meritocracy, at least where merit is measured by general cognitive skills" (p. 121).

67. See Figure 5 in text. As described in Appendix C, the regression models constructed to explain the effect of skills and schooling on earnings were able to explain between 29 and 32 percent of the total variance in cumulative earnings for each of the subgroups. The overall degree of explanatory power of the models was typically several percentage points higher for women than for men. Using step-wise regression techniques in which the effects of basic skills are estimated in the absence of all other predictors, basic skills alone explained *15 percent* of the variance or nearly half of the total explained.

68. See, for example, Chapter 3 of Jencks, et al., *Who Gets Ahead,* or Irwin Garfinkel and Sarah McLanahan, *Single Mothers and Their Children,* or Gary Solon, et al., "The Effect of Family Background on Economic Status: A Longitudinal Analysis of Sibling Correlations" (unpublished manuscript, University of Michigan, Institute for Social Research, 1987).

Past studies have found that family background variables explained between 10 and 35 percent of the variance in men's earnings. Using the PSID longitudinal data on siblings, Solon has found much larger influences. Coming from the same family explained 45 percent of the variance in earnings, 53 percent of the variance in wages, and 70 percent of the variance in educational achievement among young men.

69. See Sticht, Thomas G., *Functional Context Education* (San Diego: Applied Behavioral and Cognitive Science, Inc., March 1987), p. 29; Sticht, Thomas G., *Investing in the Education of Adults to Improve the Educability of Children* (Alexandria, Va.: Human Resources Research Organization, February 1983); Miller, Shelby, *Long Term Support for Teenage Mothers and Their Children* (Washington, D.C.: Child Welfare League of America, 1988, forthcoming); Brody, Jane E., "Child Development: Language Takes on New Significance," *The New York Times,* May 5, 1987, p. C1; Snow, Catherine E., "The Development of Conversation Between Mothers and Babies," *Journal of Child Language 4,* 1977, pp. 1–22; Snow, Catherine E., "Mothers' Speech Research: From Input to Interaction," in C. Snow and C. Ferguson (eds.), *Language Input and Acquisition* (Cambridge, Mass.: Cambridge University Press, 1977); Snow, Catherine E., "Parent-Child Interaction and the Development of Communicative Ability," in R. Schiefelbusch and J. Pickar (eds.), *Communication Competence: Acquisition and Intervention* (Baltimore: University Park Press, 1984); Baratz, Joan C., "Language in the Economically Disadvantaged Child: A Perspective," ASHA, April 1968, pp. 143–145.

Baratz discusses the then-prevalent argument that disadvantaged children have a language deficiency or "verbal destitution." She emphasizes that disadvantaged children have learned a language, but it is not standard English. Thus, they don't need remediation; they need to learn a new language. The emerging literature on language development by Snow and others seems likely to raise this controversy again.

70. *Ibid*.

71. Bumpass, Larry and Sara S. McLanahan, "The Effect of Family Structure on School Enrollment: A Comparison of Seven Racial and Ethnic Groups," Institute for Research on Poverty, Madison, Wisconsin, May 1987; McLanahan, Sara S., "Family Structure and Dependency: Early Transitions to Female Household Headship," Institute for Research on Poverty, Madison, Wisconsin, December 1986.

Female offspring who live in single-parent families at some point between the ages of twelve and sixteen were more likely to form single-mother households than their counterparts from two-parent households. Family economic status accounted for as much as 25 percent of the intergenerational effect. But even when income was controlled, daughters of single mothers were more likely to become female household heads themselves.

72. Sum, Andrew and Robert Taggart with Gordon Berlin, *Cutting Through* (New York: Ford Foundation, forthcoming).

73. The NAEP young adult literacy assessment also found that the mother's educational attainment was positively associated with mean test scores of respondents on each of the four literacy scales. Respondents in the English-speaking sample whose mothers had completed eleven or fewer years of schooling achieved mean test scores that were typically .5 to .6 standard deviations below those of respondents whose mothers had graduated from high school. Respondents whose mothers completed some postsecondary schooling obtained mean test scores one full standard deviation above those of respondents whose mothers had not graduated from high school.

74. See Heyns, Barbara, "Schooling and Cognitive Development: Is There a Season for Learning?" *Child Development,* Vol. 58, No. 5 (Chicago: University of Chicago Press, 1987); Heyns, Barbara, *Summer Learning and the Effects of Schooling* (New York: Academic Press, 1978); Heyns, Barbara, "Summer Programs and Compensatory Education: The Future of an Idea," in *Designs for Compensatory Education: Conference Proceedings and Papers,* eds. B.I. Williams, P.A. Richmond, et al., (Washington, D.C.: Research and Evaluation Association, Inc., 1987); Sipe, Cynthia L., et al., *Summer Training and Education Program (STEP): Report on the 1986 Experience* (Philadelphia: Public/Private Ventures, April 1987).

The summer-loss phenomenon has now been documented convincingly by Public/Private Ventures in the Summer Training and Education Program (STEP). STEP is a five-site random assignment experiment involving 3,000 fourteen- to fifteen-year-olds who were enrolled in either a modified summer jobs and education program or a summer jobs only program. Summer loss could be attributed to students forgetting some portion of what they learned during the school year and then falling behind as they used up a portion of the next school year's time to relearn this material. Or it could be a side effect of the test norming process in which parallel but not identical versions of a test are used to assess gains and losses. Because the P/PV data include a randomly assigned control group, large relative learning losses among controls versus experimentals provides powerful confirmation that summer loss is not solely a function of the testing, scoring, and norming process. More information on the STEP program results is provided later in this paper.

75. This appears to be true for high school youth as well in reading and basic mathematics, but less so in vocabulary and science, even when differences in course-taking are controlled for. See Rock, Donald A., et al., Chapter II, "School Level Analysis," *Study of Excellence in High School Education.*

76. Furstenberg, Frank F., J. Brooks-Gunn, and S. Philip Morgan, *Adolescent Mothers in Later Life* (Cambridge: Cambridge University Press, 1987).

77. *Ibid.,* p. 128.

78. The findings on the estimated effects of schooling and basic skills test scores on the annual earnings of young adults are based on the experiences of young men and women who were eighteen to twenty-two years old in 1979, who had completed twelve or fewer years of schooling by the time of the 1981 NLS interview, and who were *not* enrolled in school at the time of any of the 1979, 1980, and 1981 NLS interviews. The estimates of the effects of schooling and basic skills on welfare dependency, crime, and out-of-wedlock births are based on the behavior of all eighteen- to twenty-three-year-olds over the 1979 to 1981 period regardless of their educational attainment, with the exception of those still enrolled in high school. A more detailed description of the variables used in estimating these effects is provided in Appendix A and C and in Andrew Sum, et al., *Cutting Through.*

79. The completion of the twelfth grade yields a higher earnings return than any of the preceding years of high school. This effect has often been referred to as a credential effect. The total earnings impact of completing the twelfth grade is the sum of the additional year of schooling ($715) plus the diploma effect ($927), or $1,642.

80. A grade level of basic skills is equal to 4.5 points on the AFQT test, or approximately one-fourth of a standard deviation in test scores for the sample of young adults being analyzed.

81. Persons receiving cash payments under AFDC, SSI, or state-local general assistance programs and those receiving food stamps were classified as being dependent on public assistance.

82. The 1980 NLS interview questionnaire was used to collect data on prior criminal activities of respondents, including types of criminal behavior, arrests, convictions, and sentencing to correctional institutions. The arrest variable described in the text represents respondents who reported that they had been arrested one or more times for a crime other than a

minor traffic offense during the past two years. For further details on the crime variables and the probabilities of youth with varying levels of educational attainment and academic skills committing crimes see Andrew Sum and Neeta Parekh, "Criminal Behavior, Arrests, Convictions, and Sentencing of Young Adults, 19–23 Years Old in the U.S., by Sex, Race/Ethnic Group, and AFQT," Center for Labor Market Studies, Northeastern University, 1986.

83. For additional information on these estimates and their derivation, see Andrew Sum, et al., *Cutting Through*. Note that these estimates of earnings effects are of approximately the same magnitude as those found by Jencks, et al. in *Who Gets Ahead?* More importantly, these estimated effects are actually smaller then those found by John R. Berrueta-Clement, et al., *Changed Lives: The Effects of the Perry Pre-School Program on Youths Through Age 19* (Ypsilanti, Mich.: High Scope Educational Research Foundation, 1984).

84. Berrueta-Clement, et al., *Changed Lives*.

85. See Berrueta-Clement, John R., et al., *Changed Lives;* and Zigler, Edward and Winnie Berman, "Discerning the Future of Early Childhood Education," *American Psychologist,* August 1983, pp. 894–906.

The High Scope longitudinal evaluation of the Perry preschool program and related programs testing alternative curriculum approaches are among the best preschool evaluations and among the very few that used random assignment of experimental and controls and followed both groups of three- and four-year-olds through age twenty. Although other studies of exemplary preschool programs have generally confirmed the findings from the High Scope projects (see Chapter VI of *Changed Lives* for a review of six other longitudinal studies), the latter remain controversial because the small sample size (120) and the special nature of the treatment—high teacher/student ratios and home visits as well as the Ypsilanti location of the project—strike some as ungeneralizeable. Part of this controversy lies in the fact that the cognitive benefits of preschool programs, i.e., high initial IQ scores, generally disappear by grade three and age eight. Since this cognitive advantage is not sustained, most researchers are skeptical about the program's likely long-term effect on earnings and other outcomes. Most of the literature fails to note that experimental gains in achievement scores of about three-quarters of a grade level were, in fact, sustained and have grown wider over time. Since on average, effort may be more important than native ability, and achievement—what you learn—is a determinant of future life opportunities, these achievement gains are significant. Still the point remains that the Perry Preschool project is a unique high-quality model. In fact, the most recent meta-analysis (which compares results across dozens of separate experiments) of Head Start evaluation findings concludes that no educationally meaningful differences can be found on any of the Head Start evaluation studies' measures by the end of year two; see McKey, R.H. et al., *The Impact of Head Start on Children, Families and Communities* (Washington, D.C.: U.S. Department of Health and Human Services, 1985). Thus, whether high quality can be maintained in large-scale replication remains an open question. With support from the Ford Foundation and Carnegie Corporation, High Scope has begun a large-scale train-the-trainers replication effort with existing preschool programs, including Head Start educators as well as home-care providers. Results should help answer this question.

86. See Glazer, Nathan, "Education and Training Programs and Poverty," in *Fighting Poverty* (Cambridge, Mass.: Harvard University Press, 1986), pp. 153–179; Anderson, Janice, *Executive Summary Study of the Sustaining Effects of Compensatory Education* (Washington, D.C.: U.S. Department of Education, November 1981); Zagorski, Henry, et al., *Overview of Report 12: Does Compensatory Education Narrow the Achievement Gap?*, Systems Development Corporation, Santa Monica, Calif., December 1981).

87. Bell-Taylor, Wilhelmina, *Final Report on the Field Test of the Follow-Through Performance Indicator System, International Business Services, Inc.* (Washington, D.C.: U.S. Department of Education, December 1982), pp. 3-20 to 3-22.

88. The National Assessment of Educational Progress, *The Reading Report Card*.

89. Congressional Office of Technology Assessment, *Informational Technology and Its Impact on American Education* (Washington, D.C.: U.S. Government Printing Office, November 1982).

90. Goodlad, John I., *A Place Called School: Prospects for the Future* (New York: McGraw-Hill, 1983).

91. See Sipe, Cynthia L., et al., *Summer Training and Education Program: Report on the 1986 Experience* (Philadelphia: Public/Private Ventures, April 1987); Branch, Alvia, et al., *Summer Training and Education Program: Report on the 1985 Experience* (Philadelphia: Public/Private Ventures, April 1986).

92. Sipe, Cynthia L., et al., *Summer Training and Education Program: Report on the 1986 Experience*.

93. Sticht, Thomas G., et al., *Cast-Off Youth: Policy and Training Methods*

from the Military Experience (Westport, Conn.: Praeger Publishers, 1987).

94. See Sticht, Thomas G., et al., *op. cit.*; Sticht, Thomas G., *Basic Skills in Defense* (Alexandria, Va.: Human Resources Research Organization, March 1982). Figures 13–17 and pp. 34–49 of the above report contain a comprehensive summary and review of military literacy training programs, most of which were undertaken after Project 100,000.

95. See Mallar, Charles, et al., *Evaluation of the Economic Impact of the Job Corps Program, Third Follow-Up Report* (Princeton, N.J.: Mathematica Policy Research, September 1982); Team Associates, Inc., *The Job Corps' Educational Improvement Efforts* (Washington, D.C.: U.S. Department of Labor, June 1982), p. 63; Taggart, Robert, *A Fisherman's Guide: An Assessment of Remediation and Training Strategies* (Kalamazoo, Mich.: W.E. Upjohn Institute for Employment Research, 1981).

96. See Taggart, Robert, *The Comprehensive Competencies Program: A New Way to Teach, A New Way to Learn* (Washington, D.C.: Remediation and Training Institute, 1986); Taggart, Robert, *Solving the Basic Skills Crisis* (Washington, D.C.: Remediation and Training Institute, 1987).

97. See Taggart, Robert, *The Comprehensive Competencies Program: Statistics Second Quarter 1987* (Washington, D.C.: Remediation and Training Institute, August 1987).

98. Sum, Andrew, *The Longer-Term Impacts of Participation in Jobs for America's Graduates Programs: Findings of the 20-Month Follow-up of the Class of 1984* (Washington, D.C.: Jobs for America's Graduates, 1987).

99. Boyer, Ernest L., *High School: A Report on Secondary Education in America* (New York: The Carnegie Foundation for the Advancement of Education, Harper and Row, 1983).

100. Goodlad, John I., *A Place Called School.*

101. Cohen, David K., et al., *The Shopping Mall High School: Winners and Losers in the Educational Marketplace* (Boston: Houghton Mifflin, 1985).

102. Bishop, John, "Basic Skills and Worker Productivity," Draft Report, Ohio State University, Columbus, Ohio, 1985.

103. See Mathews, Jay, "Advanced Placement: Tests Help Ordinary Schools Leap Ahead," *The Washington Post*, May 14, 1987, p. 1; Mathews, Jay, "Advanced Placement—Raising the Standards: A Teacher Using Challenge of Calculus Alters Equation of Inner-City Learning," *The Washington Post*, May 15, 1987, p. 1.

104. Carnegie Forum on Education and the Economy Task Force on Teaching as a Profession, *A Nation Prepared: Teachers for the 21st Century* (New York: Carnegie Forum on Education and the Economy, 1986).

105. Shanker, Albert, "Standards Board a Bold Step Forward: Turning Point for American Education," *The New York Times,* May 17, 1987, The Week in Review, p. 7.

106. Thurow, Lester, *The Zero-Sum Solution,* Chapter 8.

107. See Taggart, Robert, "A Business Approach to Social Programming," paper prepared for the Project on Social Welfare Policy and the American Future, Ford Foundation, New York, 1987; Taggart, Robert, *A Fisherman's Guide: An Assessment of Remediation and Training Strategies.*

108. Walker, Gary, et al., *An Independent Sector Assessment of the Job Training Partnership Act, Program Year 1985* (Washington, D.C.: National Commission on Employment Policy, July 1986).

109. MDC, Inc., *The Status of Excellence in Education Commissions: Who's Looking Out for At-Risk Youth* (Chapel Hill, N.C.: MDC, Inc., 1985).

110. Brooks, Sydelle Levy with William J. Grinker, *Choice and Life Circumstances: An Ethnographic Study of Project Redirection Teens* (New York: Manpower Demonstration Research Corporation, June 1983).

111. For insights into the developmental needs of disadvantaged youth, see Lefkowitz, Bernard, *Tough Change,* Kornblum, William and Terry Williams, *Growing Up Poor* (Washington, D.C.: Lexington Books, 1985); BiHeath, Shirley and Milbrey McLaughlin, "A Child Resource Policy: Moving Beyond Dependence on School and Family," *Phi Delta Kappan,* April 1987.

112. For further evidence on the nature and size of the employment and earnings declines of young male high school dropouts, see Johnson, Clifford and Andrew Sum, *Declining Earnings of Young Men.*

113. Findings of the annual October supplement to the Current Population Survey, which tracks the school enrollment status of children, teens, and young adults, indicate that the proportion of eighteen- to twenty-four-year-olds who report having graduated from high school had not changed appreciably between 1973 and 1983, ranging between 80.1 percent and 80.9 percent. The remainder of these youth are not all high school dropouts, since a fairly high fraction of all eighteen-year-olds and a somewhat smaller fraction of nineteen-year-olds without a diploma were still enrolled in high school at the time of the October survey.

See U.S. Department of Commerce, Bureau of the Census, Figure B, *School Enrollment—Social and Economic Characteristics of Students: October 1984 (Advanced Report),* page 4.

114. BiHeath, Shirley, and Milbrey McLaughlin, ''A Child Resource Policy.''

115. Grober, David and Frazierita Davidson, ''State Employment Initiatives for Youth'' (Philadelphia: Public/Private Ventures, November 1986).

116. Glover, Robert, ''Texas Aims to be the Biggest,'' *CCP Bulletin: Fourth Quarter 1986* (Washington, D.C.: Remediation and Training Institute, p. 18).

117. Malcom, Shirley, *Equity and Excellence: Compatible Goals* (Washington, D.C: American Association for the Advancement of Science, December 1984).

The Armed Forces Qualification Test (AFQT):
Basic Skills Measures and Data Sources

The full report frequently refers to the basic academic skills of America's young adults and describes the relationship between basic skills and educational attainment, employment, earnings, childbearing, and social behavior. This appendix describes several of the specific measures used to represent the basic academic skills of young adults and the data sources for these measures.

The major data base used in the report was generated by a testing in 1980 of a nationally representative sample of approximately 12,000 American youth fifteen to twenty-three years old, including a sample of youth serving in the nation's armed forces.[1] The test used was the Armed Services Vocational Aptitude Battery, commonly referred to as the ASVAB.[2] Scores on a subset of the battery of tests comprising the ASVAB have been used to represent the basic academic skills of the nearly 12,000 teens and young adults who participated in the testing.

The ASVAB test is considered to be an aptitude test. It is used by the Department of Defense to determine eligibility for enlistment in a branch of the nation's armed services and to assign recruits to specific jobs and/or training programs. Like other aptitude tests, the ASVAB primarily measures the academic achievements of young adults at the time of testing, although it also purports to test their potential for further academic learning, performing various jobs, and successfully completing various types of military training programs.

The ASVAB test consists of ten subtests (see Figure A-1), which cover a range of academic competencies (word knowledge, reading, arithmetic reasoning, numerical operations) and knowledge in selected occupational or vocational areas, for example, information about electronics or automotive shop. Four of the subtests (word knowledge, paragraph comprehension, arithmetic reasoning, and numerical operations) are combined to form what is known as the Armed Forces Qualification Test, or the AFQT. The score on the AFQT test together with other personal background data and medical records is used to determine an individual's eligibility for enlistment. The number of test items for these four subtests is 130 and the test time is approximately 65 minutes. In determining the overall score on the AFQT test, only one-half of the test score on the numerical operations subtest is counted. Thus, the maximum score that can be obtained on the AFQT test is 105 (see Table A-1).

Figure A-1 The ten subtests of the Armed Services
Vocatibnal Aptitude Battery (ASVAB)

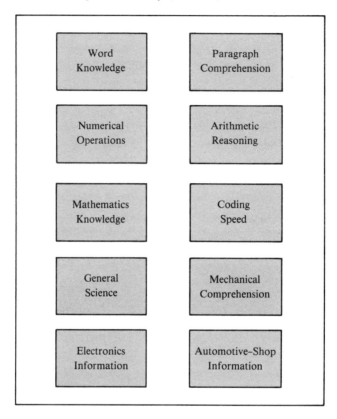

Table A-1 Sections of the AFQT test and maximum
points on each section

Section	Maximum Points
Word knowledge	35
Paragraph comprehension	15
Arithmetic reasoning	30
Numerical operations	25
Total	105

The national sample used in this report consisted of 12,693 youth (fourteen
to twenty-one years of age in 1979) who were first interviewed in 1979 as
part of the new National Longitudinal Survey of Youth Labor Market Experience (NLS).[3] The NLS survey design involved an over-sampling of black,
non-Hispanic youth; of Hispanic youth; and of non-black, non-Hispanic youth,

who were living in poverty households. Thus, sampling weights vary for different subgroups of the sample. However, the weighted data are representative of the entire non-institutional population of youth fourteen to twenty-one years old in 1979 who were living in the United States or serving overseas in a branch of the nation's armed forces. The 1980 ASVAB testing was carried out by the National Opinion Research Center at more than 400 sites throughout the nation and overseas. Tests were completed by 11,914 members of the original sample, representing a completion rate of nearly 94 percent.[4]

The NLS involves annual interviews with the original sample of 12,693 respondents. Detailed data are collected on their demographic and socioeconomic backgrounds, school attendance and educational attainment, labor-force behavior, employment and earnings experiences during each year, personal and family incomes, marital status, childbearing behavior, and criminal behavior.[5] Data from these comprehensive interviews are made available to the public by Ohio State University's Center for Human Resource Research. Tapes of the first three rounds of interviews (1979–1981) were used to generate many of the empirical findings reported in this paper on school enrollment, earnings, childbearing, and welfare dependency.

This report also contains a series of bar charts representing the distribution of young adults in various problem categories (dropouts, jobless, welfare dependent), according to their position in the AFQT test distribution for all nineteen- to twenty-three-year-olds not enrolled in high school at the time of the 1981 NLS interview. The weighted distribution of this group of young adults by AFQT test score was divided into twenty approximately equal parts, or *ventiles*. Thus, approximately 5 percent of the population of young adults is in each ventile. The AFQT test scores for each ventile are presented in Table A-2.

Table A-2   AFQT test scores, by ventile, for all 19–23-year-olds in the United States, 1981

Ventile	AFQT Test Scores	Ventile	AFQT Test Scores
Lowest	0.0–32.5	11th	78.5–80.5
2nd	33.0–41.5	12th	81.0–82.5
3rd	42.0–49.0	13th	83.0–85.0
4th	49.5–54.5	14th	85.5–87.5
5th	55.0–60.0	15th	88.0–90.0
6th	60.5–64.5	16th	90.5–92.5
7th	65.0–68.0	17th	93.0–95.0
8th	68.5–71.5	18th	95.5–97.0
9th	72.0–75.0	19th	97.5–100.0
10th	75.5–78.0	20th	100.5 and over

Notes for Appendix A

1. For a description of the purposes, design features, and findings of the 1980 ASVAB testing, see: Office of the Assistant Secretary of Defense, *Profile of American Youth: 1980 Nationwide Administration of the Armed Services Vocational Aptitude Battery,* Washington, D.C., March 1982; Sum, Andrew M., Paul Harrington, and William Goedicke, *Basic Skills of America's Teens and Young Adults: Findings of the 1980 National ASVAB Testing and Their Implications for Education, Employment and Training Policies and Programs,* report prepared for the Ford Foundation, New York, 1986.

2. For a review of the uses of the ASVAB test score data, see: Binkin, Martin, *Military Technology and Defense Manpower,* The Brookings Institution (Washington, D.C.: 1986); Sticht, Thomas G., et al., *Cast-Off Youth: Policy and Training Methods from the Military Experience,* Report prepared for the Ford Foundation, New York, February 1986; U.S. Department of Defense, *ASVAB: A Brief Guide for Counselors and Educators,* undated; U.S. Department of Defense, *ASVAB Counselor's Manual for ASVAB-14,* Washington, D.C., 1984.

3. For a description of the National Longitudinal Survey of Youth Labor Market Experience and a review of key findings from the first wave of interviews, see: Borus, Michael E., ed., *Pathways to the Future: A Report on the National Longitudinal Survey of Youth Labor Market Experience,* Youth Knowledge Development Report 2-7, U.S. Government Printing Office, Washington, D.C., 1980; Borus, Michael E., ed., *Youth and the Labor Market, Analyses of the National Longitudinal Surveys,* W.E. Upjohn Institute for Employment Research, Kalamazoo, Mich., 1984.

4. Office of the Assistant Secretary of Defense, *op. cit.,* pp. 9–13.

5. Center for Human Resource Research, *NLS Handbook, 1983* (Columbus: Ohio State University, 1983).

Literacy Proficiencies of Young Adults and High School Dropouts in the United States

Several other national testing efforts have recently made data available on the literacy proficiencies and test scores of teens and young adults with varying levels of educational attainment. Among these studies is a 1985 young adult national literacy assessment conducted by Educational Testing Service.[1] This appendix summarizes the national literacy testing results and provides information on the types of tasks that young adults with different literacy proficiencies can perform. Major emphasis is placed on the percentile rankings of youth who had failed to graduate from high school at the time of testing.

The 1985 national literacy assessment conducted by Educational Testing Service as part of the National Assessment of Educational Progress (NAEP) focused on a nationally representative sample of approximately 3,600 young adults, ages twenty-one to twenty-five. The test items were constructed to represent the types of literacy tasks that adults would encounter in everyday activities at home, at work, and in their community. The 105 separate test items were clustered to form four literacy scales referred to as Reading Proficiency, Prose Literacy, Document Literacy, and Quantitative Literacy.[2] The scores for each of the four scales were designed to have a mean of 305 and a standard deviation of 50. The entire distribution of scores for each of the four scales was examined to determine the percentile rankings for the mean score of each subgroup of respondents.

Findings on the percentile rankings of the mean scores of subgroups of respondents classified by educational attainment are summarized in Tables B-1 and B-2. A review of the findings in Tables B-1 and B-2 reveals quite

Table B-1 Percentile rankings of mean scores on each of the NAEP literacy scales, by last grade completed

Literacy Scale	0–8 Years	9–11 Years	High School Graduate, No College	Two Years College	BA or BS Degree
NAEP reading	12	14	46	74	80
Prose	14	22	42	72	82
Document utilization	10	20	42	74	83
Quantitative computation	13	22	42	71	82

Table B-2   Percentile rankings of mean scores of black and Hispanic respondents on the NAEP Reading and Literacy Scales, by years of formal
schooling completed

	Black			Hispanic		
NAEP Test	High School Dropouts	High School Graduates	4-Year College Graduates	High School Dropouts	High School Graduates	4-Year College Graduates
Reading	10	23	61	20	36	68
Prose	12	18	56	16	37	80
Document utilization	10	20	50	15	33	68
Quantitative computation	9	20	51	16	30	58

clearly the strong relationship between the literacy proficiencies of young
adults and the years of schooling they completed. Young adults who termi-
nated their formal schooling in the primary grades (one through eight) achieved
mean test scores on each of the four literacy scales, which placed them at or
near the 10th percentile. High school dropouts (nine through eleven years of
schooling) achieved mean test scores within the 14th to 22nd percentile. Black
high school dropouts tended to hover near the 10th percentile. Hispanic dropouts tended to score at or near the 15th percentile (see Table B-2).

A more complete understanding of the literacy deficiencies of young adults
lacking a high school diploma can be obtained by examining their overall
ability to answer test items correctly and the estimated probabilities of their
correctly answering particular types of questions. Young adults who completed eight or fewer years of school were able to answer correctly only 35
to 40 percent of the items on the reading, prose, and quantitative literacy
scales. Young adults with nine to eleven years of schooling were able to
answer correctly only 45 to 58 percent of the items in the same three literacy
scales. In comparison, college graduates were able to answer correctly 86
percent of the reading items, 79 percent of the prose, and 76 percent of the
quantitative items.

High school dropouts typically were able to perform well on the simple
reading and arithmetic questions, such as those involving only one task and
few or no distractors. For example, the typical high school dropout had nearly
a 90 percent probability of correctly adding two items (a check and cash) on
a bank deposit slip. When the literacy tasks involved multiple matching
features and/or distractors, the probability of completing the task correctly
fell sharply. For example, the typical high school dropout had only a 20
percent probability of successfully completing each of the following four

tasks: correctly determining how much of a tip to leave based on 10 percent of the price of a lunch, filling in a catalog order with the right individual prices and total price, estimating the per-ounce price of a jar of peanut butter, and explaining how one would go about estimating the interest charges on a loan whose terms are described in a newspaper ad.

Percentile rankings tended to rise consistently with additional years of schooling completed. Young adults who completed twelve years of schooling achieved mean test scores that placed them at the 42nd percentile on three of the four literacy scales and at the 46th percentile for the remaining scale (NAEP reading). Young adults who completed two years of college had percentile rankings in the low 70s while college graduates (B.A. or B.S. degree) achieved mean test scores in the low 80s. Although blacks and Hispanics tended to obtain mean test scores below those of whites, regardless of educational attainment, the patterns of the relationships between test scores and school attainment were quite similar to those for all young adults. The percentile rankings of black and Hispanic graduates from four-year colleges and universities were typically 30 to 40 percentage points above those of high school graduates and 40 to 50 percentage points above those of dropouts. Clearly, minorities with the strongest literacy proficiencies are the ones who graduate from four-year colleges and universities.

Notes for Appendix B

1. For a description of the design of this testing effort, see Kirsch, Irwin S. and Ann Jungeblut, *Literacy: Profiles of America's Young Adults, Final Report* (Princeton, N.J.: Educational Testing Service, 1986).
2. For further details on the construction of these literacy scales, see: Kirsch, Irwin S. and Ann Jungeblut, "Chapter 3: Defining and Anchoring the Literacy Scales," *op. cit.*

**Estimates of the Independent Effects of
Additional Years of Secondary Schooling and
Higher Basic Skills Test Scores on the Earnings
of Young Adults in the United States**

Discussions within the body of this report and the data presented in Table 3 in the text indicate that young men and women who graduated from high school and who had higher levels of basic academic skills tended to obtain higher annual earnings. The average annual earnings of those who graduated from high school exceeded earnings of high school dropouts by fairly sizeable margins; the annual earnings gaps existed even when the two groups possessed comparable levels of basic academic skills. For both high school graduates and high school dropouts, annual earnings tend to rise fairly uniformly with higher levels of tested basic academic skills as measured by scores on the AFQT (see Table 3 in the text).

All of the estimates appearing in Table 3 were based on data generated by the first three rounds of interviews with a nationally representative sample of young adults selected to participate in the National Longitudinal Survey of Youth Labor Market Experience (NLS).[1] The annual average earnings estimates are *unadjusted data;* that is, they represent the actual earnings experiences of the sample of young men and women. Some portion of the estimated earnings differences between high school graduates and high school dropouts and between respondents with higher and lower levels of tested basic skills is attributable to factors other than formal schooling and better basic skills. For example, male high school graduates are more likely than male dropouts to be white, to live outside the South, to have parents with higher levels of formal schooling, and to have lived with both of their parents when they were teenagers.

To isolate the independent effects of additional years of secondary schooling and higher tested basic academic skills on the earnings of respondents, we constructed and estimated the parameters of a series of multiple regression models designed to explain variations in the cumulative earnings of our sample of respondents over a three-year period, calendar years 1978 to 1980. Such models (using nearly identical explanatory variables) were designed to explain variations in the earnings of all men and all women separately and of key subgroups of men and women classified by their racial or ethnic groups and by their parents' educational attainment. Earnings regressions were estimated for fourteen such subgroups of men and women (seven each).

As noted, these multivariate regression models were used to generate estimates of the *independent effects* of additional years of secondary schooling and higher basic skills proficiencies on the earnings of our sample of young men and women. The dependent variable in each of these models was the *cumulative earnings* of respondents over the 1978 to 1980 calendar year period. Our earnings variable represented the sum of earnings from civilian

Table C-1 Independent variables appearing in the regression models of cumulative earnings

■ Adjusted age variable that takes into account the age of the respondent and the number of years of schooling completed.

■ Race or ethnic group of the respondent. Two dichotomous variables representing whether a respondent was black, non-Hispanic, or Hispanic.

■ Health status of the respondent. Two dichotomous variables representing whether a respondent had a health problem that limited the type of work he or she could perform or that prevented him or her from working.

■ Criminal conviction status of the respondent. A continuous variable representing the number of times the respondent had been convicted of a crime other than a minor traffic offense by the time of the 1980 interview.

■ Marital status of respondent. Two dichotomous variables representing the marital status of the respondent over the entire 1978–80 period.

■ Number of children borne or fathered by the respondent. A continuous variable representing the annual average number of children that the respondent had either borne or fathered up to the date of the 1979 to 1981 interviews.

■ Educational attainment of the respondent. Three dichotomous variables representing the number of years of schooling completed by the respondent at the time of the 1981 NLS interview.

■ Basic academic skills of the respondent. A continuous variable representing the actual AFQT test score of the respondent minus the mean AFQT test score for all eighteen- to twenty-three-year-old high school graduates and dropouts in the United States.

■ Family background of the respondent. Variables included two dichotomous variables representing the educational attainment of the respondent's parents and one variable representing the presence of both parents in the home of the respondent at age fourteen.

■ Region of the residence of respondent. A dichotomous variable representing whether the respondent lived in the South at age fourteen.

■ Local economic conditions in the area in which the respondent resided. A continuous variable representing the average unemployment rate in the local area in which the respondent resided over the 1978–80 period.

wage and salary employment, from self-employment, and from service in the armed forces.[2] This cumulative earnings variable was regressed against a series of eighteen variables representing current demographic and socioeconomic characteristics of respondents, their health status, their criminal arrest records, their educational attainment, their AFQT scores, their family background, and the labor market conditions in the local areas in which they resided during 1978, 1979, and 1980.[3] A list and brief description of each of these independent variables is presented in Table C-1.

Findings of the Effects of Schooling and Basic Skills on Earnings

The results of the regression analysis have been analyzed and used to generate a comprehensive set of estimates of the independent effects of additional years of secondary schooling and higher basic skills on the cumulative earnings of respondents. Our findings are summarized in Tables C-2, C-3, and C-4. We have generated estimates of the *predicted earnings differences* between high school dropouts with varying levels of schooling and basic academic skills and high school graduates. These predicted earnings differences are based on the estimated coefficients of the schooling and AFQT score variables for each subgroup of respondents.[4]

For both men and women, we provide six estimates of the predicted size of the earnings differences. The first three estimates across each row involve comparisons of the predicted earnings differences between high school graduates and those with nine or fewer years of schooling. The second set of estimates are based on a comparison of differences between high school graduates and those with eleven years of schooling.[5] For each of these two groups, we also provide estimates of the expected size of the earnings differences assuming no difference in AFQT scores, a twenty-point difference in AFQT scores, and a forty-point difference. Twenty points is equivalent to a one standard deviation difference in the scores of two groups. Overall, our sample of high school graduates achieved a mean AFQT score approximately one full standard deviation above that of all high school dropouts. A two standard deviation difference in an AFQT test score is equivalent to comparing someone in the top 20 percent of the distribution to someone in the bottom 20 percent.

The findings in Table C-2 reveal quite clearly that completing high school and having solid basic academic skills had substantive independent effects on the earnings of young adults in American labor markets in the 1978–80 period. With all other factors constant, male high school graduates obtained mean cumulative earnings over the three-year period that were $13,930 above those of their counterparts with nine or fewer years of schooling. This earnings difference was equivalent to 56 percent of the mean earnings of our entire

Table C-2 Estimated three-year cumulative earnings advantages of high school graduates with no college versus high school dropouts, by years of schooling completed, basic skills gaps, and sex

| | Earnings Advantages | | | | | |
| | Graduates vs. Dropouts with 9 or fewer years of school | | | Graduates vs. Dropouts with 11 years of school | | |
Sex	Same AFQT	20 pts. Higher	40 pts. Higher	Same AFQT	20 pts. Higher	40 pts. Higher
Males						
Absolute size	$13,930	$17,311	$20,692	$2,600	$5,980	$9,361
As percent of mean for all males	56.3	69.9	83.6	10.5	24.2	37.8
Females[a]						
Absolute size	$2,297	$4,937	$7,577	$2,297	$4,937	$7,577
As percent of mean for all females	18.9	40.6	62.2	18.9	40.6	62.2

Note: Data are for persons 20–23 years of age in 1981.

[a] These estimates are derived after controlling for the effects of all other variables listed in Table C-1, including the effect of basic skills. When basic skills are controlled, completing the tenth or eleventh grade rather than the ninth grade does not add significantly to the earnings of women. Thus when basic skills are taken into account, no relative earnings difference exists between women who have completed the ninth versus the tenth or eleventh grade of school. As a result, the earnings differences between female graduates and high school dropouts with nine or fewer years of school are the same as those for graduates versus dropouts with eleven or fewer years of school.

sample of men. When these graduates also had basic skills one standard deviation above those of the dropouts, their mean earnings were $17,311 higher, or 70 percent of the mean earnings level for this sample of men. A two-standard deviation in AFQT scores in favor of the male high school graduate would have led to a predicted earnings difference of $20,692, or 84 percent of the mean earnings level.

The predicted differences between the cumulative earnings of male high school graduates and male high school dropouts with eleven years of schooling are sharply lower than those for dropouts with fewer years of schooling; however, they still remain fairly large, particularly when accompanied by basic skills advantages. For example, holding all other factors constant including AFQT scores, male high school graduates had predicted mean earnings that were $2,600 higher than those for male dropouts with eleven years of schooling, a difference equal to 10.5 percent of the mean earnings of men. When these graduates also had a twenty-point AFQT score advantage, we predict that they would have earned $5,980 more than dropouts with eleven years of schooling, an advantage equal to 24 percent of the mean earnings level for men.

Young women who completed high school and possessed above-average basic academic skills also had earnings well above those of female high school dropouts with limited basic skills. For example, holding all other factors including AFQT scores constant, female high school graduates obtained mean cumulative earnings that were approximately $2,300 above those of comparable women with eleven years of schooling. The absolute size of the earnings advantage rises to $4,937 when the diploma is accompanied by a one-standard deviation basic skills advantage. Even though the absolute sizes of these mean predicted earnings differences for female high school graduates are below those of male high school graduates, their relative sizes are higher than those of men due to the lower mean cumulative earnings of women. During the 1978–80 period, the mean cumulative earnings of women were approximately only half of those of men ($12,200 versus $24,750).[6]

To determine whether the possession of a high school diploma and solid basic academic skills would favorably affect the expected earnings of key subgroups of males and females, separate regression models were estimated for race or ethnic groups and for young adults from different family backgrounds as measured by their parents' educational attainment. Key findings for men are summarized in Table C-3 and for women in Table C-4.

The findings on the effects of schooling and skills are consistently positive for all subgroups of young men and women. Particularly promising results are those for black men and women and for young adults whose parents had not graduated from high school. On average, black men and women tended to obtain the highest absolute and relative returns from more years of schooling and better basic skills. For example, in comparison to the earnings of their counterparts with eleven years of schooling and AFQT test scores twenty points lower, the relative sizes of the predicted cumulative earnings advantages for male high school graduates were 42.4, 20.0, and 13.8 percent for black, white, and Hispanic males, respectively. The comparable estimates for female high school graduates were 77.4, 65.9, and 29.7 percent, respectively, for black, Hispanic, and white females. Minority youth who complete high school and possess solid basic academic skills tend to *substantially* out-earn their counterparts with limited skills who fail to complete high school.

The estimates appearing in the bottom half of Tables C-3 and C-4 also indicate that young adult men and women whose parents had limited educational attainment (less than high school) frequently tended to benefit the most from completing high school and acquiring solid basic academic skills. Compared to their counterparts who did not complete high school, young

Table C-3 Estimated three-year cumulative earnings advantages of male high school graduates with no college versus male high school dropouts, with eleven years of schooling completed, by size of basic skills gaps, race/ethnic group, and parents' education

Variable	Earnings Advantages		
	Same AFQT Score	20 points Higher	40 points Higher
White, non-Hispanic			
Absolute size	$2,188	$5,374	$8,560
Percent of mean	8.1	20.0	31.9
Black, non-Hispanic			
Absolute size	$4,689	$6,525	$8,361
Percent of mean	30.5	42.4	54.3
Hispanic			
Absolute size	$1,000	$2,760	$4,520
Percent of mean	5.0	13.8	22.6
Neither parent a high school graduate			
Absolute size	$4,122	$6,873	$9,624
Percent of mean	19.3	32.1	45.0
One or both parents a high school graduate			
Absolute size	$1,464	$4,092	$6,720
Percent of mean	5.4	15.0	24.7
One or both parents with some postsecondary schooling			
Absolute size	$0	$4,638	$9,662
Percent of mean	0.0	18.8	39.2

Note: Data are for persons 20–23 years of age in 1981.

high school graduates whose parents had not graduated from high school had the highest relative earnings gains. For example, the relative size of the earnings advantages of male high school graduates with a twenty-point AFQT score advantage were 32, 15, and 19 percent, respectively, for those whose parents had not graduated from high school, whose parents had graduated from high school, and whose parents had completed some postsecondary schooling.[7] For women, the relative sizes of these earnings advantages in favor of high school graduates with above-average basic skills were 63.7, 52.4, and 26.5 percent, respectively.

Thus, the findings for both young male and female adults reveal that completing high school and acquiring strong basic academic skills are effective

Table C-4   Estimated three-year cumulative earnings advantages of female high school graduates with no college versus female high school dropouts, by size of basic skills gaps, race/ethnic group, and parents' education

Variable	Earnings Advantages		
	Same AFQT	20 points Higher	40 points Higher
White, non-Hispanic			
Absolute size	$1,599	$3,911	$6,223
Percent of mean	12.1	29.7	47.2
Black, non-Hispanic			
Absolute size	$4,432	$7,101	$9,770
Percent of mean	48.3	77.4	106.4
Hispanic			
Absolute size	$3,782	$6,617	$9,452
Percent of mean	37.7	65.9	94.1
Neither parent a high school graduate			
Absolute size	$3,264	$6,304	$9,344
Percent of mean	33.0	63.7	94.4
One or both parents a high school graduate			
Absolute size	$4,474	$6,976	$9,478
Percent of mean	33.6	52.4	71.2
One or both parents with some postsecondary schooling			
Absolute size	$3,577	$3,817	$4,057
Percent of mean	24.8	26.5	28.1

Note: Data are for persons 20–23 years of age in 1981.

strategies for substantively raising the potential earnings of young adults who do not go on to college. Such strategies appear to be particularly effective for minority youth and for young adults whose parents had limited educational attainment.

Notes for Appendix C

1. The earnings estimates appearing in Table 3 are based on weighted observations for sample respondents. The sample consists of young men and women who were eighteen years of age or older at the time of the first NLS interview in 1979, who had completed twelve or fewer years of school at the time of the 1981 interview, and who were not enrolled in school at the time of any of the first three interviews.

2. Only those respondents for whom complete annual earnings data were available for the years 1978, 1979, and 1980 were included in our regression analysis. Such earnings data were available for approximately 90 percent of our sample of twenty- to twenty-three-year-olds with twelve or fewer years of schooling.

3. Each of the regression models typically was able to explain between 29 and 32 percent of the total variance in cumulative earnings for each of the subgroups. The overall degree of explanatory power of the models was typically several percentage points higher for women than for men. Using step-wise regression techniques in which the effects of basic skills are estimated in the absence of all other predictors, basic skills alone explained *15 percent* of the variance, or nearly half of the total explained.

4. In nearly all cases, the coefficient on the high school graduation and AFQT score variables were statistically significant at the .01 level. In two cases, the value of the coefficient on the high school graduation variable was significant only at the .10 level.

5. The definition of a high school graduate used in conducting this analysis is a person who reported that he or she had completed exactly twelve years of schooling by the time of the 1981 NLS interview. Not all persons completing twelve years of school possess a high school diploma; however, our analysis of the 1979 NLS interview data revealed that approximately 99 percent of those reporting twelve years of schooling claimed that they possessed a high school diploma, a GED degree, or both.

6. The mean earnings data included those with zero earnings in any given year. Earnings differences between men and women were influenced by differences in mean weeks worked. About one-third of the higher mean earnings of men was attributable to higher mean weeks of employment during this three-year period.

7. These educational attainment classifications were made on the basis of a review of the educational attainment of both the father and mother of the respondent. The first category contains respondents, neither of whose parents graduated from high school. The second group contains respondents, one or both of whose parents graduated from high school, but did not complete any postsecondary schooling. The last group of respondents consisted of those who had one or both parents completing some postsecondary schooling.

Gordon Berlin is Deputy Director of the Urban Poverty
Program, Ford Foundation, New York, N.Y.

Andrew Sum is Associate Professor, Department of
Economics, Northeastern University.